Strange Stories from

Young People

George Cary Eggleston

Alpha Editions

This edition published in 2024

ISBN : 9789362995469

Design and Setting By
Alpha Editions
www.alphaedis.com
Email - info@alphaedis.com

Contents

PREFACE.

In calling the tales in this volume "Strange Stories" I have sought simply to indicate that, in the main, they are unfamiliar to youthful readers, and that most of them relate deeds and occurrences some what out of the common. In choosing the themes I have tried to avoid the tales that have been often used, and to tell only those of which young readers generally have not before heard.

Of course, a book of this kind can make no pretension to originality of matter, as the facts used in it are to be found in historical works of recognized authority, though many of them have been drawn from books that are not easily accessible to the majority of readers. If there is any originality in my little volume it is in the manner in which the tales are told. I have endeavored to tell them as simply as possible, and at the same time with as much dramatic force and fervor as I could command, while adhering rigidly to the facts of history.

It would be impossible for me to say to what sources I am indebted for materials. The incidents related have been familiar to me for years, as they are to all persons whose reading of history has been at all extensive, and I cannot say with any certainty how much of each I learned from one and how much from another historical writer. Nor is it in any way necessary that I should do so, as the recorded facts of history are common property. But a special acknowledgment is due to Mr. James Parton in the case of the tale of the Negro Fort, and also for certain details in those relating to the New Orleans campaign of 1814-15. In that field Mr. Parton is an original investigator, to whose labors every writer on the subject must be indebted. I wish also to acknowledge my obligation to Mr. A. B. Meek, the author of a little work entitled "Romantic Passages in Southwestern History," for the main facts in the stories of the Charge of the Hounds and the Battle of the Canoes on the Alabama River; but, with respect to those matters, I have had the advantage of private sources of information also.

Most of the stories in the volume were originally written for *Harper's Young People*; one was first published in *Good Cheer*, and a few in other periodicals. I owe thanks to the editors and publishers concerned for permission to reprint them in this form.

THE STORY OF THE NEGRO FORT.

During the war of 1812-14, between Great Britain and the United States, the weak Spanish Governor of Florida—for Florida was then Spanish territory—permitted the British to make Pensacola their base of operations against us. This was a gross outrage, as we were at peace with Spain at the time, and General Jackson, acting on his own responsibility, invaded Florida in retaliation.

Among the British at that time was an eccentric Irish officer, Colonel Edward Nichols, who enlisted and tried to make soldiers of a large number of the Seminole Indians. In 1815, after the war was over, Colonel Nichols again visited the Seminoles, who were disposed to be hostile to the United States, as Colonel Nichols himself was, and made an astonishing treaty with them, in which an alliance, offensive and defensive, between Great Britain and the Seminoles, was agreed upon. We had made peace with Great Britain a few months before, and yet this ridiculous Irish colonel signed a treaty binding Great Britain to fight us whenever the Seminoles in the Spanish territory of Florida should see fit to make a war! If this extraordinary performance had been all, it would not have mattered so much, for the British government refused to ratify the treaty; but it was not all. Colonel Nichols, as if determined to give us as much trouble as he could, built a strong fortress on the Appalachicola River, and gave it to his friends the Seminoles, naming it "The British Post on the Appalachicola," where the British had not the least right to have any post whatever. Situated on a high bluff, with flanks securely guarded by the river on one side and a swamp on the other, this fort, properly defended, was capable of resisting the assaults of almost any force that could approach it; and Colonel Nichols was determined that it should be properly defended, and should be a constant menace and source of danger to the United States. He armed it with one 32-pounder cannon, three 24-pounders, and eight other guns. In the matter of small-arms he was even more liberal. He supplied the fort with 2500 muskets, 500 carbines, 400 pistols, and 500 swords. In the magazines he stored 300 quarter casks of rifle powder and 763 barrels of ordinary gunpowder.

When Colonel Nichols went away, his Seminoles soon wandered off, leaving the fort without a garrison. This gave an opportunity to a negro bandit and desperado named Garçon to seize the place, which he did, gathering about him a large band of runaway negroes, Choctaw Indians, and other lawless persons, whom he organized into a strong company of robbers. Garçon made the fort his stronghold, and began to plunder the country round about as thoroughly as any robber baron or Italian bandit ever did, sometimes venturing across the border into the United States.

All this was so annoying and so threatening to our frontier settlements in Georgia, that General Jackson demanded of the Spanish authorities that they should reduce the place; and they would have been glad enough to do so, probably, if it had been possible, because the banditti plundered Spanish as well as other settlements. But the Spanish governor had no force at command, and could do nothing, and so the fort remained, a standing menace to the American borders.

Matters were in this position in the spring of 1816, when General Gaines was sent to fortify our frontier at the point where the Chattahoochee and Flint rivers unite to form the Appalachicola. In June of that year some stores for General Gaines's forces were sent by sea from New Orleans. The vessels carrying them were to go up the Appalachicola, and General Gaines was not sure that the little fleet would be permitted to pass the robbers' stronghold, which had come to be called the Negro Fort. Accordingly, he sent Colonel Clinch with a small force down the river, to render any assistance that might be necessary. On the way Colonel Clinch was joined by a band of Seminoles, who wanted to recapture the fort on their own account, and the two bodies determined to act together.

Meantime the two schooners with supplies and the two gun-boats sent to guard them had arrived at the mouth of the river; and when the commandant tried to hold a conference with Garçon, the ship's boat, bearing a white flag, was fired upon.

Running short of water while lying off the river's mouth, the officers of the fleet sent out a boat to procure a supply. This boat was armed with a swivel and muskets, and was commanded by Midshipman Luffborough. The boat went into the mouth of the river, and, seeing a negro on shore, Midshipman Luffborough landed to ask for fresh-water supplies. Garçon, with some of his men, lay in ambush at the spot, and while the officer talked with the negro the concealed men fired upon the boat, killing Luffborough and two of his men. One man got away by swimming, and was picked up by the fleet; two others were taken prisoners, and, as was afterwards learned, Garçon coated them with tar and burned them to death.

It would not do to send more boats ashore, and so the little squadron lay together awaiting orders from Colonel Clinch. That officer, as he approached the fort, captured a negro, who wore a white man's scalp at his belt, and from him he learned of the massacre of Luffborough's party. There was no further occasion for doubt as to what was to be done. Colonel Clinch determined to reduce the fort at any cost, although the operation promised to be a very difficult one.

Placing his men in line of battle, he sent a courier to the fleet, ordering the gun-boats to come up and help in the attack. The Seminoles made many demonstrations against the works, and the negroes replied with their cannon. Garçon had raised his flags—a red one and a British Union-jack—and whenever he caught sight of the Indians or the Americans, he shelled them vigorously with his 32-pounder.

Three or four days were passed in this way, while the gun-boats were slowly making their way up the river. It was Colonel Clinch's purpose to have the gun-boats shell the fort, while he should storm it on the land side. The work promised to be bloody, and it was necessary to bring all the available force to bear at once. There were no siege-guns at hand, or anywhere within reach, and the only way to reduce the fort was for the small force of soldiers—numbering only one hundred and sixteen men—to rush upon it, receiving the fire of its heavy artillery, and climb over its parapets in the face of a murderous fire of small-arms. Garçon had with him three hundred and thirty-four men, so that, besides having strong defensive works and an abundant supply of large cannon, his force outnumbered Colonel Clinch's nearly three to one. It is true that the American officer had the band of Seminoles with him, but they were entirely worthless for determined work of the kind that the white men had to do. Even while lying in the woods at a distance, waiting for the gun-boats to come up, the Indians became utterly demoralized under the fire of Garçon's 32-pounder. There was nothing to be done, however, by way of improving the prospect, which was certainly hopeless enough. One hundred and sixteen white men had the Negro Fort to storm, notwithstanding its strength and the overwhelming force that defended it. But those one hundred and sixteen men were American soldiers, under command of a brave and resolute officer, who had made up his mind that the fort could be taken, and they were prepared to follow their leader up to the muzzle of the guns and over the ramparts, there to fight the question out in a hand-to-hand struggle with the desperadoes inside.

Finally the gun-boats arrived, and preparations were made for the attack. Sailing-master Jairus Loomis, the commandant of the little fleet, cast his anchors under the guns of the Negro Fort at five o'clock in the morning on the 27th of July, 1816. The fort at once opened fire, and it seemed impossible for the little vessels to endure the storm of shot and shell that rained upon them from the ramparts above. They replied vigorously, however, but with no effect. Their guns were too small to make any impression upon the heavy earthen walls of the fortress.

Sailing-master Loomis had roused his ship's cook early that morning, and had given him a strange breakfast to cook. He had ordered him to make all the fire he could in his galley, and to fill the fire with cannon-balls. Not long after the bombardment began the cook reported that breakfast was ready; that is to say, that the cannon-balls were red-hot. Loomis trained one of his guns with his own hands so that its shot should fall within the fort, instead of burying itself in the ramparts, and this gun was at once loaded with a red-hot shot. The word was given, the match applied, and the glowing missile sped on its way. A few seconds later the earth shook and quivered, a deafening roar stunned the sailors, and a vast cloud of smoke filled the air, shutting out the sun.

The hot shot had fallen into the great magazine, where there were hundreds of barrels of gunpowder, and the Negro Fort was no more. It had been literally blown to atoms in a second.

The slaughter was frightful. There were, as we know already, three hundred and thirty-four men in the fort, and two hundred and seventy of them were killed outright by the explosion. All the rest, except three men who miraculously escaped injury, were wounded, most of them so badly that they died soon afterwards.

One of the three men who escaped the explosion unhurt was Garçon himself. Bad as this bandit chief was, Colonel Clinch would have spared his life, but it happened that he fell into the hands of the sailors from the gun-boat; and when they learned that Garçon had tarred and burned their comrades whom he had captured in the attack on Luffborough's boat, they turned him over to the infuriated Seminoles, who put him to death in their own cruel way.

BREAKFAST AND BATTLE.

This is the history of a strange affair, which at one time promised to give the government of the United States no little trouble, even threatening to involve us in a war with Spain, for the fort was on Spanish territory, and the Spaniards naturally resented an invasion of their soil.

A WAR FOR AN ARCHBISHOP.

THE CURIOUS STORY OF VLADIMIR THE GREAT.

In the latter part of the tenth century Sviatozlaf was Grand Prince of Russia. He was a powerful prince, but a turbulent one, and he behaved so ill towards his neighbors that, when an opportunity offered, one of them converted his skull into a gold-mounted drinking-cup, with an inscription upon it, and his dominions were parcelled out between his three sons— Yaropolk, Oleg, and Vladimir.

Yaropolk, finding his possessions too small for his ambition, made war on Oleg, and conquered his territory; but his brother Oleg having been killed in the war, the tender-hearted Yaropolk wept bitterly over his corpse.

The other brother, Vladimir, was so grieved at the death of Oleg that he abandoned his capital, Novgorod, and remained for a time in seclusion. Yaropolk seized the opportunity thus offered, and made himself master of Vladimir's dominions also. Not long afterwards Vladimir appeared at the head of an army, and Yaropolk ran away to his own capital, Kiev. Vladimir at once resumed the throne, and sent word to Yaropolk that he would in due time return the hostile visit.

About this time Yaropolk and Vladimir both asked for the hand of the Princess Rogneda, of Polotzk, in marriage; and the father of the princess, fearing to offend either of the royal barbarians, left the choice to Rogneda herself. She chose Yaropolk, sending a very insulting message to Vladimir, whereupon that prince marched against Polotzk, conquered the province, and with his own hand slew the father and brothers of the princess. Then, with their blood still unwashed from his hands, he forced Rogneda to marry him.

Having attended to this matter, Vladimir undertook to return his brother's hostile visit, as he had promised to do. Yaropolk's capital, Kiev, was a strongly fortified place, and capable of a stout resistance; but Vladimir corrupted Blude, one of Yaropolk's ministers, paying him to betray his master, and promising, in the event of success, to heap honors on his head. Blude worked upon Yaropolk's fears, and persuaded him to abandon the capital without a struggle, and Vladimir took possession of the throne and the country. Even in his exile, however, Yaropolk had no peace. Blude frightened him with false stories, and persuaded him to remove from place to place, until his mind and body were worn out, when, at Blude's suggestion, he determined to surrender himself, and trust to the mercy of

Vladimir. That good-natured brother ordered the betrayed and distressed prince to be put to death.

Then Vladimir rewarded Blude. He entertained him in princely fashion, declaring to his followers that he was deeply indebted to this man for his faithful services, and heaping all manner of honors upon him. But at the end of three days he said to Blude: "I have kept my promise strictly. I have received you with welcome, and heaped unwonted honors upon your head. This I have done as your friend. To-day, as judge, I condemn the traitor and the murderer of his prince." He ordered that Blude should suffer instant death, and the sentence was executed.

Now that both Oleg and Yaropolk were dead, Vladimir was Grand Prince of all the Russias, as his father before him had been. He invaded Poland, and made war upon various others of his neighbors, greatly enlarging his dominions and strengthening his rule.

But Vladimir was a very pious prince in his heathen way, and feeling that the gods had greatly favored him, he made rich feasts of thanksgiving in their honor. He ordered splendid memorials to various deities to be erected throughout the country, and he specially honored Perune, the father of the gods, for whom he provided a new pair of golden whiskers—golden whiskers being the special glory of Perune.

Not content with this, Vladimir ordered a human sacrifice to be made, and selected for the victim a Christian youth of the capital. The father of the boy resisted, and both were slain, locked in each other's arms.

Vladimir gave vast sums of money to the religious establishments, and behaved generally like a very devout pagan. His piety and generosity made him so desirable a patron that efforts were made by the priests of other religions to convert him. Jews, Mohammedans, Catholics, and Greeks all sought to win him, and Vladimir began seriously to consider the question of changing his religion. He appointed a commission, consisting of ten boyards, and ordered them to examine into the comparative merits of the different religions, and to report to him. When their report was made, Vladimir weighed the matter carefully.

He began by rejecting Mohammedanism, because it forbids the use of wine, and Vladimir was not at all disposed to become a water-drinker. Judaism, he said, was a homeless religion, its followers being wanderers on the face of the earth, under a curse; so he would have nothing to do with that faith. The Catholic religion would not do at all, because it recognized in the pope a superior to himself, and Vladimir had no mind to acknowledge a superior. The Greek religion was free from these objections, and moreover, by adopting it he would bring himself into friendship with the great Greek or

Byzantine Empire, whose capital was at Constantinople, and that was something which he earnestly desired to accomplish.

Accordingly, he determined to become a Christian and a member of the Greek Church; but how? There were serious difficulties in the way. In order to become a Christian he must be baptized, and he was puzzled about how to accomplish that. There were many Greek priests in his capital, any one of whom would have been glad to baptize the heathen monarch, but Vladimir would not let a mere priest convert him into a Christian. Nobody less than an archbishop would do for that, and there was no archbishop in Russia.

It is true that there were plenty of archbishops in the dominions of his Byzantine neighbors, and that the Greek emperors, Basil and Constantine, would have been glad to send him a dozen of them if he had expressed a wish to that effect; but Vladimir was proud, and could not think of asking a favor of anybody, least of all of the Greek emperors. No, he would die a heathen rather than ask for an archbishop to baptize him.

Nevertheless, Vladimir had fully made up his mind to have himself baptized by an archbishop. It was his lifelong habit, when he wanted anything, to take it by force. He had taken two thirds of his dominions in that way, and, as we have seen, it was in that way that he got his wife Rogneda. So now that he wanted an archbishop, he determined to take one. Calling his army together, he declared war on the Greek emperors, and promising his soldiers all the pillage they wanted, he marched away towards Constantinople.

The first serious obstacle he met with was the fortified city of Kherson, situated near the spot where Sebastopol stands in our day. Here the resistance was so obstinate that month after month was consumed in siege operations. At the end of six months Vladimir became seriously alarmed lest the garrison should be succored from without, in which case his hope of getting himself converted into a Christian must be abandoned altogether.

While he was troubled on this score, however, one of his soldiers picked up an arrow that had been shot from the city, and found a letter attached to it. This letter informed the Grand Prince that the water-pipes of the city received their supplies at a point immediately in his rear, and with this news Vladimir's hope of becoming a Christian revived. He found the water-pipes and stopped them up, and the city surrendered.

There were plenty of bishops and archbishops there, of course, and they were perfectly willing—as they had been from the first, for that matter—to baptize the unruly royal convert, but Vladimir was not content now with that. He sent a messenger to Constantinople to tell the emperors there that he wanted their sister, the Princess Anne, for a wife; and that if they refused, he would march against Constantinople itself. The Emperors Basil and Constantine consented, and although Vladimir had five wives already, he married Anne, and was baptized on the same day.

Having now become a Christian, the Grand Prince determined that his Russians should do the same. He publicly stripped the god Perune of his gorgeous golden whiskers, and of his rich vestments, showing the people that Perune was only a log of wood. Then he had the deposed god whipped in public, and thrown into the river, with all the other gods.

He next ordered all the people of his capital city to assemble on the banks of the Dnieper River, and, at a signal, made them all rush into the water, while a priest pronounced the baptismal service over the whole population of the city at once. It was the most wholesale baptism ever performed.

0

VLADIMIR BESIEGING THE CITY CONTAINING HIS ARCHBISHOP.

That is the way in which Russia was changed from a pagan to a Christian empire. The story reads like a romance, but it is plain, well-authenticated history. For his military exploits the Russian historians call this prince Vladimir the Great. The people call him St. Vladimir, the Greek Church having enrolled his name among the saints soon after his death. He was undoubtedly a man of rare military skill, and unusual ability in the government of men. Bad as his acts were, he seems to have had a conscience, and to have done his duty so far as he was capable of understanding it.

THE BOY COMMANDER OF THE CAMISARDS.

When Louis XIV. was King of France, that country was generally Catholic, as it is still, but in the rugged mountain region called the Cevennes more than half the people were Protestants. At first the king consented that these Protestant people, who were well behaved both in peace and in war, should live in quiet, and worship as they pleased; but in those days men were not tolerant in matters of religion, as they are now, and so after a while King Louis made up his mind that he would compel all his people to believe alike. The Protestants of the Cevennes were required to give up their religion and to become Catholics. When they refused, soldiers were sent to compel them, and great cruelties were practised upon them. Many of them were killed, many put in prison, and many sent to work in the galleys.

When this persecution had lasted for nearly thirty years, a body of young men who were gathered together in the High Cevennes resolved to defend themselves by force. They secured arms, and although their numbers were very small, they met and fought the troops.

Among these young men was one, a mere boy, named Jean Cavalier. His home was in the Lower Cevennes, but he had fled to the highlands for safety. This boy, without knowing it, had military genius of a very high order, and when it became evident that he and his comrades could not long hold out against the large bodies of regular troops sent against them, he suggested a plan which in the end proved to be so good that for years the poor peasants were able to maintain war against all the armies that King Louis could send against them, although he sent many of his finest generals and as many as sixty thousand men to subdue them.

Cavalier's plan was to collect more men, divide, and make uprisings in several places at once, so that the king's officers could not tell in which way to turn. As he and his comrades knew the country well, and had friends to tell them of the enemy's movements, they could nearly always know when it was safe to attack, and when they must hide in the woods.

Cavalier took thirty men and went into one part of the country, while Captain La Porte, with a like number, went to another, and Captain St. John to still another. They kept each other informed of all movements, and whenever one was pressed by the enemy, the others would begin burning churches or attacking small garrisons. The enemy would thus be compelled to abandon the pursuit of one party in order to go after the others, and it soon became evident that under Cavalier's lead the peasants were too wily and too strong for the soldiers. Sometimes Cavalier would fairly beat detachments of his foes, and give them chase, killing all whom he caught; for in that war both sides did this, even killing their prisoners without mercy. At other times Cavalier was worsted in fight, and when that was the case he fled to the woods, collected more men, and waited for another chance.

Without trying to write an orderly history of the war, for which there is not space enough here, I shall now tell some stories of Cavalier's adventures, drawing the information chiefly from a book which he himself wrote years afterwards, when he was a celebrated man and a general in the British army.

One Sunday Cavalier, who was a preacher as well as a soldier, held services in his camp in the woods, and all the Protestant peasants in the neighborhood attended. The Governor of Alais, whose name was De la Hay, thought this a good opportunity not only to defeat Cavalier's small force, but also to catch the Protestant women and children in the act of attending a Protestant service, the punishment for which was death. He collected a force of about six hundred men, cavalry and infantry, and marched towards the wood, where he knew he should outnumber the peasants three or four to one. He had a mule loaded with ropes, declaring that he was going to hang all the rebels at once.

When news of De la Hay's coming was brought to the peasants, they sent away all the country people, women, and children, and began to discuss the situation. They had no commander, for although Cavalier had led them generally, he had no authority to do so. Everything was voluntary, and everything a subject of debate. On this occasion many thought it best to retreat at once, as there were less than two hundred of them; but Cavalier declared that if they would follow him, he would lead them to a place where victory might be won. They consented, and he advanced to a point on the road where he could shelter his men. Quickly disposing them in line of battle behind some defences, he awaited the coming of the enemy.

De la Hay, being over-confident because of his superior numbers, blundered at the outset. Instead of attacking first with his infantry, he placed his horsemen in front, and ordered an assault. Cavalier was quick to take advantage of this blunder. He ordered only a few of his men to fire, and this drew a volley from the advancing horsemen, which did little damage to the sheltered troops, but emptied the horsemen's weapons. Instantly Cavalier ordered a charge and a volley, and the horsemen, with empty pistols, gave way, Cavalier pursuing them. De la Hay's infantry, being just behind the horsemen, were ridden down by their own friends, and became confused and panic-stricken. Cavalier pursued hotly, his men throwing off their coats to lighten themselves, and giving the enemy no time to rally. A reinforcement two hundred strong, coming up, tried to check Cavalier's charge; but so impetuous was the onset that those fresh troops gave way in their turn, and the chase ended only when the king's men had shut themselves up in the fortified towns. Cavalier had lost only five or six men, the enemy losing a hundred killed and many more wounded. Cavalier captured a large quantity of arms and ammunition, of which he was in sore need.

When the battle was over it was decided unanimously to make Cavalier the commander. He refused, however, to accept the responsibility unless it could be accompanied with power to enforce obedience, and his troops at once voted to make his authority absolute, even to the decision of questions of life and death. According to the best authorities, Cavalier was only seventeen years old when this absolute command was conferred upon him. How skilfully he used the scant means at his disposal we shall see hereafter.

On one occasion Cavalier attacked a party of forty men who were marching through the country to reinforce a distant post, and killed most of them. While searching the dead bodies, he found in the pocket of the commanding officer an order signed by Count Broglio, the king's lieutenant, directing all military officers and town authorities to lodge and feed the party on their march. No sooner had the boy soldier read this paper than he resolved to turn it to his own advantage in a daring and dangerous way.

The castle of Servas, near Alais, had long been a source of trouble to him. It was a strong place, built upon a steep hill, and was so difficult of approach that it would have been madness to try to take it by force. This castle stood right in the line of Cavalier's communications with his friends, near a road which he was frequently obliged to pass, and its presence there was a source of annoyance and danger to him. Moreover, its garrison of about forty men were constantly plundering and murdering Cavalier's friends in the country round about, and giving timely notice to his enemies of his own military movements.

When he found the order referred to, he resolved to pretend that he was Count Broglio's nephew, the dead commander of the detachment which he had just destroyed. Dressing himself in that officer's clothes, he ordered his men to put on the clothing of the other dead royalists. Then he took six of his best men, with their own Camisard uniforms on, and bound them with ropes, to represent prisoners. One of them had been wounded in the arm, and his bloody sleeve helped the stratagem. Putting these six men at the head of his troop, with a guard of their disguised comrades over them, he marched towards the Castle of Servas. There he declared himself to be Count Broglio's nephew, and said that he had met a company of the

Barbets, or Camisards, and had defeated them, taking six prisoners; that he was afraid to keep these prisoners in the village overnight lest their friends should rescue them; and that he wished to lodge them in the castle for safety. When the governor of the castle heard this story, and saw the order of Count Broglio, he was completely imposed upon. He ordered the prisoners to be brought into the castle, and invited Cavalier to be his guest there for the night. Taking two of his officers with him, Cavalier went into the castle to sup with the governor. During supper several of his soldiers, who were encamped just outside, went into the castle upon pretence of getting wine or bread, and when five or six of them were in, at a signal from Cavalier, they overpowered the sentinels and threw the gates open. The rest of the troop rushed in at once, and before the garrison could seize their arms the boy commander was master of the fortress. He put the garrison to the sword, and, hastily collecting all the arms, ammunition, and provisions he could find, set fire to the castle and marched away. When the fire reached the powder magazine the whole fortress was blown to fragments, and a post which had long annoyed and endangered the Camisards was no more.

CAVALIER PERSONATING THE LIEUTENANT OF THE COUNT BROGLIO.

On another occasion, finding himself short of ammunition, Cavalier resolved to take some by force and stratagem from the strongly fortified town of Savnes. His first care was to send a detachment of forty men to a point at some distance, with orders to burn a church which had lately been fortified, "thereby," he says, "to make the inhabitants of Savnes believe we were busy in another place." Then he detached an officer and fifty men, and ordered them to disguise themselves as country militia in the king's service, and to go into Savnes in that character. With some difficulty this officer accomplished his purpose, and then Roland and Cavalier marched upon the place. His officer inside the town, when the alarm was given, said to the governor, "Let them come; you'll see how I'll receive them." Anxious for his own safety, the governor permitted the supposed officer of militia to take charge of the defence, and the armed citizens put themselves under his command. He instructed the citizens to reserve their fire until he should give them orders, and in that way enabled Cavalier to approach unharmed. Suddenly the officer, directing the aim of his men against the citizens, ordered them to throw down their arms upon pain of instant death, and they, seeing themselves caught in a trap, obeyed. Cavalier marched in without opposition, secured all that he could carry away of arms, ammunition, and provisions, and retired to the woods.

Throughout the summer and autumn the boy carried on his part of the war, nearly always getting the better of his enemies by his shrewdness and valor, and when that was impossible, eluding them with equal shrewdness. During that first campaign he destroyed many fortified places, won many fights against superior numbers of regular troops, and killed far more soldiers for the enemy than he had under his own command. Failing to conquer him by force or strategy, his foes fell back upon the confident hope of starving him during the winter, for he must pass the winter in the forests, with no bases of supply to draw upon for either food or ammunition. But in indulging this hope his enemies forgot that the crown and glory of his achievements in the field had been his marvellous fertility of resource. The very qualities which had made him formidable in fight were his safeguard for the winter. He knew quite as well as they did that he must live all winter in the woods surrounded by foes, and, knowing the difficulty of doing so, he gave his whole mind to the question of how to do it.

He began during the harvest to make his preparations. He explored all the caves in the mountains, and selected the most available ones for use as magazines, taking care to have them in all parts of the mountains, so that if cut off from one he could draw upon another. In these caves he stored great quantities of grain and other provisions, and during the winter, whenever he needed meal, some of his men, who were millers, would carry grain to some lonely country mill and grind it. To prevent this, the king's officers ordered that all the country mills should be disabled and rendered unfit for use; but before the order could be executed, Cavalier directed some of his men, who were skilled machinists, to disable two or three of the mills by carrying away the essential parts of their machinery and storing them in his caves. Then, when he wanted meal, his machinists had only to replace the machinery in some disabled mill, and remove it again after his millers had done the necessary grinding. His bakers made use of farmers' ovens to bake bread in, and when the king's soldiers, hearing of this, destroyed the ovens, Cavalier sent his masons—for he had all sorts of craftsmen in his ranks—to rebuild them.

Having two powder-makers with him, he collected saltpetre, burned willow twigs for charcoal, and made all the powder he needed in his caves. Before doing so he had been obliged to resort to many devices in order to get powder, sometimes disguising himself as a merchant and going into a town and buying small quantities at a time, so that suspicion might not be awakened, until he secured enough to fill his portmanteau.

For bullets he melted down the leaden weights of windows, and when that source of supply failed he melted pewter vessels and used pewter bullets—a fact which gave rise to the belief that he used poisoned balls. Finally, in a dyer's establishment, he had the good luck to find two great leaden kettles, weighing more than seven hundred quintals, which, he says, "I caused immediately to be carried into the magazines with as much diligence and care as if they had been silver."

Chiefly by Cavalier's tireless energy and wonderful military skill, the war was kept up against fearful odds for years, and finally the young soldier succeeded in making a treaty of peace in which perfect liberty of conscience and worship—which was all he had been fighting for—was guaranteed to the Protestants of the Cevennes. His friends rejected this treaty, however, and Cavalier soon afterwards went to Holland, where he was given command of a regiment in the English service. His career in arms was a brilliant one, so brilliant that the British made him a general and governor of the island of Jersey; but he nowhere showed greater genius or manifested higher soldierly qualities than during the time when he was the Boy Commander of the Camisards.

THE CANOE FIGHT.

AN INCIDENT OF THE CREEK WAR.

The smallest naval battle ever fought in the world, perhaps, occurred on the Alabama River on the 13th of November, 1813, between two canoes, and this is the way in which it happened.

The United States were at war with Great Britain at that time, and a war with Spain was also threatened. The British had stirred up the Indians in the Northwest to make war upon the whites, and in 1813 they persuaded the Creek Indians of Alabama and Mississippi to begin a war there.

The government troops were so busy with the British in other quarters of the country that very little could be done for the protection of the white settlers in the Southwest, and for a good while they had to take care of themselves in the best way they could. Leaving their homes, they gathered together here and there and built rude stockade forts, in which they lived, with all their women and children. All the men, including all the boys who were old enough to pull a trigger—and frontier boys learn to use a gun very early in life—were organized into companies of volunteer soldiers.

At Fort Madison, one of the smallest of the forts, there was a very daring frontiersman, named Samuel (or Sam) Dale—a man who had lived much with the Indians, and was like them in many respects, even in his dress and manners. Hearing that the Indians were in force on the southeastern bank of the Alabama River, the people in Fort Madison were greatly alarmed, fearing that all the crops in that region—which were ripe in the fields— would be destroyed. If that should occur, they knew they must starve during the coming winter, and so they made up their minds to drive the savages away, at least until they could gather the corn.

Captain Dale at once made up a party, consisting of seventy-two men, all volunteers. With this force he set out on the 11th of November, taking Tandy Walker, a celebrated scout, for his guide. The column marched to the Alabama River, and crossed it at a point about twenty miles below the present town of Claiborne.

Once across the river, Dale knew that he was among the Indians, and, knowing their ways, he was as watchful as if he had been one of them himself. He forbade his men to sleep at all during the night after crossing the river, and kept them under arms, in expectation of an attack.

No attack being made, he moved up the river the next morning, marching most of the men, but ordering Jerry Austill, with six men, to paddle up in two canoes that had been found. This Jerry Austill—who afterwards became a merchant in Mobile and a state senator—was a boy only nineteen years of age at the time, but he had already distinguished himself in the war by his courage.

At a point called Peggy Bailey's Bluff, Dale, who was marching with one man several hundreds of yards ahead of his men, came upon a party of Indians at breakfast. He shot one of them, and the rest ran away, leaving their provisions behind them. Securing the provisions, Dale marched on for a mile or two, but, finding no further trace of Indians, he concluded that the country on that side of the river was now pretty clear of them, and so he set to work to cross to the other side, meaning to look for enemies there.

The river at that point is about a quarter of a mile wide, and, as there were only two small canoes at hand, the work of taking the men across was very slow. When all were over except Dale and about a dozen others, the little remnant of the force was suddenly attacked.

The situation was a very dangerous one. With the main body of his command on the other side of the river, where it could give him no help, Dale had to face a large body of Indians with only a dozen men, and, as only one canoe remained on his side of the river, it was impossible for the whole of the little party to escape by flight, as the canoe would not hold them all.

Concealing his men in the bushes, behind trees, and under the river-bank, he replied to the fire of the Indians, and kept them at bay. But it was certain that this could not last long. The Indians must soon find out from the firing how small the number of their adversaries was; and Dale knew that as soon as the discovery was made, they would rush upon him, and put the whole party to death.

He called to the men on the other side of the river to come over and help him, but they were panic-stricken, probably because they could see, as Dale could not, how large a body of Indians was pressing their commander. The men on the other bank did, indeed, make one or two slight attempts to cross, but those came to nothing, and the little party on the eastern shore seemed doomed to destruction.

Bad as matters were with Dale, they soon became worse. An immense canoe, more than thirty feet long and four feet deep, came down the river, bearing eleven warriors, who undertook to land and attack Dale in the rear. This compelled the party to fight in two directions at once. Dale and his companions kept up the battle in front, while Jerry Austill, James Smith, and one other man fought the warriors in the canoe to keep them from landing. One of the eleven was killed, and another swam ashore and succeeded in joining the Indians on the bank.

Seeing how desperate the case was, Dale resolved upon a desperate remedy. He called for volunteers for a dangerous piece of work, and was at once joined by Jerry Austill, James Smith, and a negro man whose name was Cæsar. With these men he leaped into the little canoe, and paddled towards the big Indian boat, meaning to fight the nine Indians who remained in it, although he and his canoe party numbered only four men all told.

As the two canoes approached each other, both parties tried to fire, but their gunpowder was wet, and so they grappled for a hand-to-hand battle. Jerry Austill, being in front, received the first attack. No sooner did the two canoes touch than an Indian sprang forward, and dealt the youth a terrible blow with a war-club, knocking him down, and making a dent in his skull which he carried through life. Once down, he would have been killed but for the quickness of Smith, who, seeing the danger his companion was in, raised his rifle. With a single blow he knocked over the Indian with whom Austill was struggling.

Then Austill rose, and the fierce contest went on. Dale and his men rained their blows upon their foes, and received blows quite as lusty in return, but Cæsar managed the boat so skilfully that, in spite of the superior numbers of the Indians, the fight was not very unequal. He held the little boat against the big one, but kept it at the end, so that the Indians in the other end of the big canoe could not reach Dale's men.

In this way those that were actually fighting Dale, Austill, and Smith never numbered more than three or four at any one time, and so the three could not be borne down by mere force of numbers. Dale stood for a time with one foot in each boat; then he stepped over into the Indian canoe, giving his comrades more room, and crowding the Indians towards the end of their boat.

One by one the savages fell, until only one was left facing Dale, who held Cæsar's gun, with bayonet attached, in his hand. This sole survivor was Tar-cha-chee, an Indian with whom Dale had hunted and lived, one whom he regarded as a friend, and whom he now wished to spare. But the savage was strong within the Indian's breast, and he refused to accept mercy even from a man who had been his comrade and friend. Standing erect in the bow of the canoe, he shook himself, and said, in the Muscogee tongue, "Big Sam, you are a man, I am another; now for it."

With that he rushed forward, only to meet death at the hands of the friend who would gladly have spared him.

"WITH A SINGLE BLOW HE KNOCKED OVER THE INDIAN WITH WHOM AUSTILL WAS STRUGGLING."

The canoe fight was ended, but Dale's work was not yet done. His party on the bank were every minute more closely pressed, and if they were to be saved it must be done quickly. For this purpose he and his companions at once began clearing the big canoe of its load of dead Indians. Now that only the white men were there, the Indians upon the bank directed a galling fire upon the canoe, but by careening it to one side Dale made a sort of breastwork of its thick gunwale, and thus succeeded in clearing it. When this was done he went ashore and quickly carried off the party there, landing all of them in safety on the other side.

The hero of this singular battle lived until the year 1841. The whole story of his life is a romance of hardship, daring, and wonderful achievement. When he died, General John F. H. Claiborne, who knew him intimately, wrote a sketch of his career for a Natchez newspaper, in which he described him as follows:

"In person General Dale was tall, erect, raw-boned, and muscular. In many respects, physical and moral, he resembled his antagonists of the woods. He had the square forehead, the high cheek-bones, the compressed lips, and, in fact, the physiognomy of an Indian, relieved, however, by a firm, benevolent Saxon eye. Like the red men, too, his foot fell lightly upon the ground, and turned neither to the right nor left. He was habitually taciturn, his face grave, he spoke slowly and in low tones, and he seldom laughed. I observed of him what I have often noted as peculiar to border men of high attributes: he entertained the strongest attachment for the Indians, extolled their courage, their love of country, and many of their domestic qualities;

and I have often seen the wretched remnant of the Choctaws camped round his plantation and subsisting on his crops."

It is a curious fact that after the war ended, when Weatherford (Red Eagle), who commanded the Indians on the shore in this battle with Dale, was about to marry, he asked Dale to act as his best man, and the two who had fought each other so desperately stood side by side, as devoted friends, at the altar.

THE BATTLE OF LAKE BORGNE.

HOW THE BRITISH MADE A LANDING UNDER DIFFICULTIES.

When the British made up their minds, near the end of the year 1814, to take New Orleans, and thus to get control of the Mississippi River, there seemed to be very little difficulty in their way.

So far as anybody on either side could see, their only trouble was likely to be in making a landing. If they could once get their splendid army on shore anywhere near the city, there was very little to prevent them from taking the town, and if they had taken it, it is easy to see that the whole history of the United States would have been changed.

They did make a landing, but they did not take New Orleans, and in the story of "The Battle in the Dark" I shall tell how and why they failed. In the present story I want to tell how they landed.

The expedition consisted of a large fleet bearing a large army. At first the intention was to sail up the Mississippi River, but General Jackson made that impossible by building strong forts on the stream, and so it was necessary to try some other plan.

It happens that New Orleans has two entrances from the sea. The river flows in front of the city, and by that route it is about a hundred miles from the city to the sea; but just behind the town, only a few miles away, lies a great bay called Lake Pontchartrain. This bay is connected by a narrow strait with another bay called Lake Borgne, which is connected directly with the sea.

Lake Borgne is very shallow, but the British knew little about it. They only knew that if they could land anywhere on the banks of Lake Borgne or Lake Pontchartrain they would be within an easy march of New Orleans.

Accordingly, the fleet bearing the British army, instead of entering the mouth of the Mississippi, and trying to get to New Orleans in front, sailed in by the back way, and anchored near the entrance of Lake Borgne.

Here the British had their first sight of the preparations made to resist them. Six little gun-boats, carrying twenty-three guns in all, were afloat on the lake under command of Lieutenant Thomas Ap Catesby Jones. These gun-boats were mere mosquitoes in comparison with the great British men-of-war, and when they made their appearance in the track of the invading fleet, the British laughed and wondered at the foolhardiness of the American commander in sending such vessels there.

Lieutenant Thomas Ap Catesby Jones knew what he was about, however, as the British soon found out. He sailed up almost within cannon-shot of the enemy's ships, and they, of course, gave chase to him. Then he nimbly sailed away, with the fleet after him. Very soon a large man-of-war ran aground; then another and another struck the bottom, and the British Admiral began to understand the trick. It was evident that Lake Borgne was much too shallow for the large ships, and so the commander called a halt, and transferred the troops to the smaller vessels of the fleet.

When that was done the chase was begun again by the smaller ships, and for a time with every prospect of success; but presently even these ships were hard aground, and the whole British fleet which had been intended to carry the army across the lake was stuck fast in the mud near the entrance, and thirty miles from the point at which the landing was to be made.

The British commander was at his wits' end. It was clear that the ships could not cross the lake, and the only thing to be done was to transport the army across little by little in the ships' boats, and make a landing in that way. But to do that while Lieutenant Jones and his gun-boats were afloat was manifestly impossible. If it had been attempted, the little gun-boats, which could sail anywhere on the lake, would have destroyed the British army by boat-loads.

There was nothing to be done until the saucy little fleet was out of the way, and to put it out of the way was not easy.

Lieutenant Jones was an officer very much given to hard fighting, and in this case the British saw that they must fight him at a disadvantage. As they could not get to him in their ships, they must make an attack in open boats, which, of course, was a very dangerous thing to do, as the American gun-boats were armed with cannon.

The British commander wanted his bravest men for such work, and so he called for volunteers to man the boats. A thousand gallant fellows offered themselves, and were placed in fifty boats, under command of Captain Lockyer. Each boat was armed with a carronade—a kind of small cannon—but the men well knew that the real fighting was not to be done with carronades. The only hope of success lay in a sudden, determined attack. The only way to capture the American gun-boats was to row up to them in the face of their fire, climb over their sides, and take them by force in a hand-to-hand fight.

BOARDING THE GUN-BOATS.

When the flotilla set sail, on the 14th of December, Lieutenant Jones knew what their mode of attack would be quite as well as Captain Lockyer did. If he let them attack him in the open lake he knew very well that the British could overpower him and capture his fleet; but he did not intend to be attacked in the open lake if he could help it. His plan was to sail slowly, keeping just out of reach of the row-boats, and gradually to draw them to the mouth of the strait which leads into Lake Pontchartrain. At that point there was a well-armed fort, and if he could anchor his gun-boats across the narrow channel, he believed he could destroy the British flotilla with the aid of the fort, and thus beat off the expedition from New Orleans.

Unluckily, while the fleet was yet far from the mouth of the strait the wind failed entirely, and the gun-boats were helpless. They could not sail without wind, and they must receive the attack right where they were.

At daylight on the morning of December 15 the British flotilla was about nine miles away, but was rapidly drawing nearer, the boats being propelled by oars. Lieutenant Jones called the commanders of his gun-boats together, gave them instructions, and informed them of his purpose to make as obstinate a fight as possible. His case was hopeless; his fleet would be captured, but by fighting obstinately he could at least gain time for General Jackson at New Orleans, and time was greatly needed there.

Meanwhile the British boats, carrying a thousand men, all accustomed to desperate fighting, approached and anchored just out of gunshot. Captain Lockyer wished his men to go into action in the best condition possible, and therefore he came to anchor in order to rest the oarsmen, and to give the men time for breakfast.

At half-past ten o'clock the British weighed anchor, and, forming in line, began the advance. As soon as they came within range the American gun-boats opened fire, but with little effect at first. Of course the British could not reply at such a distance, but being under fire, their chief need was to go forward as fast and come to close quarters as quickly as possible. The sailors bent to their oars, and the boats flew over the water. Soon the men at the bows began to fire the carronades in reply to the American cannon. Then as the boats drew nearer, small arms came into use, and the battle grew fiercer with every moment. The British boats were with difficulty kept in line, and their advance grew slower. Oarsmen were killed, and time was lost in putting others into their places. Still the line was preserved, and the battle went on, the attacking boats slowly and steadily advancing all the time.

Two of the American gun-boats had drifted out of place, and were considerably in advance of the rest. Seeing this, Captain Lockyer ordered the men commanding the British boats to surround them, and a few minutes later the sailors were climbing over the sides of these vessels. Their attack was stoutly resisted. The American sailors above them fired volleys into their faces, and beat them back with handspikes. Scores of the British fell back into the water dead or wounded, while their comrades pressed forward to fill their places. There were so many of them that in spite of all the Americans could do to beat them off they swarmed over the gunwales and gained the decks. Their work was not yet done, however. The Americans fiercely contested every inch of their advance, and the two parties hewed each other down with cutlasses, the Americans being slowly beaten back by superior numbers, but still obstinately fighting until they could fight no more.

One by one all the gun-boats were taken in this way, Lieutenant Jones's vessel holding out longest, and the Lieutenant himself fighting till he was stricken down with a severe wound.

Having thus cleared Lake Borgne, the British were free to begin the work of landing. It was a terrible undertaking, however—scarcely less so than the fight itself. The whole army had to be carried thirty miles in open boats and landed in a swamp. The men were drenched with rain, and, a frost coming on, their clothes were frozen on their bodies. There was no fuel to be had on the island where they made their first landing, and to their sufferings from cold was added severe suffering from hunger before supplies of food could be brought to them. Some of the sailors who were engaged in rowing the boats were kept at work for four days and nights without relief.

The landing was secured, however, and the British cared little for the sufferings it had cost them. They believed then that they had little more to do except to march twelve miles and take possession of the city, with its one hundred and fifty thousand bales of cotton and its ten thousand hogsheads of sugar. How it came about that they were disappointed is made clear in the next story.

THE BATTLE IN THE DARK.

HOW GENERAL JACKSON RECEIVED THE BRITISH.

When the British succeeded in taking Lieutenant Jones's little gun-boats and making a landing, after the manner described in the preceding story, they supposed that the hardest part of their work was done. It was not far from their landing-place to New Orleans, and there was nothing in their way. Their army numbered nearly twenty thousand men, and the men were the best soldiers that England had. Many of them were Wellington's veterans.

It seemed certain that such an army could march into New Orleans with very little trouble indeed, and everybody on both sides thought so—everybody, that is to say, but General Jackson. He meant to fight that question out, and as the Legislature and many of the people in the city would do nothing to help him, he put the town under martial law, and worked night and day to get together something like an army.

On the 23d of December, 1814, the British arrived at a point a few miles below the city, and went into camp about noon. As soon as Jackson heard of their arrival he said to the people around him, "Gentlemen, the British are below: we must fight them tonight."

He immediately ordered his troops forward. He had made a soldier of everybody who could carry a gun, and his little army was a curiously mixed collection of men. There were a few regulars, in uniform; there were some Mississippi troopers, and Coffee's Kentucky and Tennessee hunters, in hunting-shirts and jeans trousers; there were volunteers of all sorts from the streets of New Orleans—merchants, lawyers, laborers, clerks, and clergymen—armed with shot-guns, rifles, and old muskets; there were some criminals whom Jackson had released from prison on condition that they would fight; there was a battalion of free negroes, who were good soldiers; and, finally, there were about twenty Choctaw Indians.

GENERAL JACKSON AT NEW ORLEANS.

With this mixed crowd Jackson had to fight the very best troops in the British army. Only about half of his men had ever heard a bullet whistle, and less than half of them were drilled and disciplined; but they were brave men who believed in their general, and they were about to fight for their country as brave men should. When all were counted—backwoodsmen, regulars, city volunteers, negroes, Indians, and all—the whole army numbered only 2131 men! But, weak as this force was, Jackson had made up his mind to fight with it. He knew that the British were too strong for him, but he knew too that every day would make them stronger, as more and more of their troops would come forward each day.

The British camp was nine miles below the city, on a narrow strip of land between the river and a swamp. Jackson sent a gun-boat, the *Carolina*, down the river, with orders to anchor in front of the camp and pour a fire of grape-shot into it. He sent Coffee across to the swamp, and ordered him to creep through the bushes, and thus get upon the right flank of the British. He kept the rest of his army under his own command, ready to advance from the front upon the enemy's position.

But no attack was to be made until after dark. The army was kept well out of sight, and the British had no suspicion that any attack was thought of. They did not regard Jackson's men as soldiers at all, but called them a *posse comitatus* of ragamuffins—that is to say, a mob of ragged citizens—and the most they expected such a mob to do was to wait somewhere below the city until the British soldiers should get ready to drive them away with a few volleys.

So the British lighted their camp-fires, stacked their arms for the night, and cooked their suppers. They meant to stay where they were for a day or two until the rest of their force could come up, and then they expected to march into the town and make themselves at home.

Night came on, and it was exceedingly dark. At half-past seven o'clock there came a flash and a roar. The *Carolina*, lying in the river, within a few hundred yards of the camp, had begun to pour her broadsides into the British quarters. Her cannon vomited fire, and sent a hail-storm of grape-shot into the camp, while the marines on board kept up a steady fire of small-arms.

The British were completely surprised, but they were cool-headed old soldiers, who were not to be scared by a surprise. They quickly formed a line on the bank, and, bringing up some cannon, gave battle to the saucy gun-boat.

For ten minutes this fight went on between the Americans on the river and the British on shore; then Jackson ordered his troops to advance. His columns rushed forward and fell upon the enemy, again surprising them, and forcing them to fight on two sides at once. Coffee, who was hidden over in the swamp, no sooner heard the roar of the *Carolina's* guns than he gave the word to advance, and, rushing out of the bushes, his rough Tennesseeans and Kentuckians attacked still another side of the enemy's position.

Still the sturdy British held their ground, and fought like the brave men and good soldiers that they were. It was too dark for anybody to see clearly what was going on. The lines on both sides were soon broken up into independent groups of soldiers, who could not see in what direction they were marching, or maintain anything like a regular fight. Regiments and battalions wandered about at their own discretion, fighting whatever bodies of the enemy they met, and sometimes getting hopelessly entangled with each other. Never was there so complete a jumble on a battle-field. Whenever two bodies of troops met, they had to call out to each other to find out whether they were friends or foes; then, if one body proved to be Americans and the other British, they delivered a volley, and rushed upon each other in a desperate struggle for mastery.

Sometimes a regiment would win success in one direction, and just as its enemy on that side was driven back, it would be attacked from the opposite quarter. Coffee's men were armed with squirrel rifles, which, of course, had no bayonets; but the men had their long hunting-knives, and with no better weapons than these they did not hesitate to make charge after charge upon the lines of gleaming bayonets.

The British suffered terribly from the first, but their steadiness was never lost for a moment. The mad onset of the Americans broke their lines, and in the darkness it was impossible to form them again promptly; but still the men kept up the fight, while the officers, as rapidly as they could, directed their detached columns towards protected positions.

Retreating slowly and in as good order as they could, the British got beyond the range of the *Carolina's* guns by nine o'clock, and, finding a position where a bank of earth served for a breastwork, they made a final stand there. It was impossible to drive them from such a position, and so, little by little, the Americans withdrew, and at ten o'clock the Battle in the Dark was at an end.

Now let us see what Jackson had gained or lost by this hasty attack. The British were still in a position to threaten New Orleans. They had not been driven away, and the rest of their large army, which had not yet come up, was hurrying forward to help them. They had lost a great many more men than Jackson had, but they could spare men better than he could, and they were not whipped by any means. Still, the attack was equal to a victory for the Americans. It is almost certain that if Jackson had waited another day before fighting he would have lost New Orleans, and the whole Southwest would have been overrun.

But, by making this night attack, he showed the British that he could and would fight; and they, finding what kind of a defence he meant to make, made up their minds to move slowly and cautiously. They waited for the rest of their force to come up, and while they were waiting and getting ready Jackson had more than two weeks' time in which to collect troops from the country north of him, to get arms and ammunition, and to throw up strong fortifications. When the British made their grand attack on the 8th of January, 1815, they found Jackson ready for them. His army was increased, his men were full of confidence, and, best of all, he had a line of strong earth-works to fight behind. It is commonly said that his fortifications were made of cotton-bales, but that is an error. When he first began to fortify, he used some cotton-bales, and some sugar, which, it was thought, would do instead of sand; but in some of the early skirmishes it was found that the sugar was useless, because it would not stop cannon-balls; while the cotton was worse, because it took fire, and nearly suffocated the men behind it with smoke. The cotton and sugar were at once thrown aside, and the battle of New Orleans was fought behind earth-works. In that battle the British were so badly worsted that they gave up all idea of taking New Orleans, which, a month before, they had believed it would be so easy to capture.

THE TROUBLESOME BURGHERS.

Philip van Artevelde was a Dutchman. His father, Jacob, had been Governor of Ghent, and had made himself a great name by leading a revolt against the Count of Flanders, and driving that tyrant out of the country on one occasion.

Philip was a quiet man, who attended to his own affairs and took no part in public business; but in the year 1381 the good people of Ghent found themselves in a very great difficulty. Their city was subject to the Count of Flanders, who oppressed them in every way. He and his nobles thought nothing of the common people, but taxed them heavily and interfered with their business.

The city of Bruges was the rival of Ghent, and in those days rivals in trade were enemies. The Bruges people were not satisfied with trying to make more money and get more business than Ghent could, but they wanted Ghent destroyed, and so they supported Count Louis in all that he did to injure their neighboring city.

Having this quarrel on their hands, the Ghent people did not know what to do. Count Louis was too strong for them, and they were very much afraid he would destroy their town and put the people to death.

A public meeting was held, and remembering how well old Jacob van Artevelde had served them against the father of Count Louis, they made his son Philip their captain, and told him he must manage this quarrel for them.

Philip undertook this duty, and tried to settle the trouble in some peaceable way; but the Count was angry, and would not listen to anything that Van Artevelde proposed. He said the Ghent people were rebels, and must submit without any conditions at all, and this the sturdy Ghent burghers refused to do.

Count Louis would not march against the town and give the people a fair chance to fight the matter out. He preferred to starve them, and for that purpose he put soldiers on all the roads leading towards Ghent, and refused to allow any provisions to be taken to the city.

The people soon ate up nearly all the food they had, and when the spring of 1382 came they were starving. Something must be done at once, and Philip van Artevelde decided that it was of no use to resist any longer. He took twelve deputies with him, and went to beg the Count for mercy. He offered to submit to any terms the Count might propose, if he would only promise not to put any of the people to death. Philip even offered himself as a victim, agreeing that the Count should banish him from the country as a punishment, if he would spare the people of the town. But the haughty Count would promise nothing. He said that all the people of Ghent from fifteen to sixty years old must march half-way to Bruges bareheaded, with no clothes on but their shirts, and each with a rope around his neck, and then he would decide how many of them he would put to death and how many he would spare.

The Count thought the poor Ghent people would have to submit to this, and he meant to put them all to death when they should thus come out without arms to surrender. He therefore called on his vassals to meet him in Bruges at Easter, and to go out with him to "destroy these troublesome burghers."

But the "troublesome burghers," as we shall see presently, were not the kind of men to walk out bareheaded, with ropes around their necks, and submit to destruction.

Philip van Artevelde returned sadly to Ghent, on the 29th of April, and told the people what the Count had said. Then the gallant old soldier Peter van den Bossche exclaimed:

"In a few days the town of Ghent shall be the most honored or the most humbled town in Christendom."

Van Artevelde called the burghers together, and told them what the situation was. There were 30,000 people in Ghent, and there was no food to be had for them. There was no hope that the Count would offer any better terms, or that anybody would come to their assistance. They must decide quickly what they would do, and Philip said there were three courses open to them. First, if they chose, they could wall up the gates of the town and die of starvation. Secondly, they could accept the Count's terms, march out with the ropes around their necks, and take whatever punishment the Count might put upon them. If they should decide to do that, Philip said he would offer himself to the Count to be hanged first. Thirdly, they could get together 5000 of their best men, march to Bruges, and fight the quarrel out.

The answer of the people was that Philip must decide for them, and he at once said, "Then we will fight."

The 5000 men were got together, and on the 1st of May they marched out of the town to win or lose the desperate battle. The priests of the city stood at the gates as the men marched out, and prayed for blessings upon them. The old men, the women, and the children cried out, "If you lose the battle you need not return to Ghent, for you will find your families dead in their homes."

The only food there was for these 5000 men was carried in five little carts, while on another cart two casks of wine were taken.

The next day Van Artevelde placed his little army in line on the common of Beverhoutsveld, at Oedelem, near Bruges. There was a marsh in front of them, and Van Artevelde protected their flank by a fortification consisting of the carts and some stakes driven into the ground. He then sent a messenger to the Count, begging him to pardon the people of Ghent, and, having done this, he ordered his men to go to sleep for the night.

At daybreak the next morning the little army was aroused to make final preparations for the desperate work before them. The priests exhorted the men to fight to the death, showing them how useless it would be to surrender or to run away, as they were sure to be put to death at any rate. Their only hope for life was in victory, and if they could not win that, it would be better to die fighting like men than to surrender and be put to death like dogs.

After these exhortations were given, seven gray friars said mass and gave the sacrament to all the soldiers. Then the five cart-loads of provisions and the two casks of wine were divided among the men, for their last breakfast. When that meal was eaten, the soldiers of Ghent had not an ounce of food left anywhere.

Meanwhile the Count called his men together in Bruges, and got them ready for battle; but the people of Bruges were so sure of easily destroying the little Ghent army that they would not wait for orders, but marched out shouting and singing and making merry.

THE BURGHERS PREPARE TO DEFEND THEIR CITY.

As their column marched along the road in this noisy fashion, the "troublesome burghers" of Ghent suddenly sprang upon them, crying, "Ghent! Ghent!"

The charge was so sudden and so fierce that the Bruges people gave way, and fled in a panic towards the town, with Van Artevelde's men at their heels in hot pursuit. The Count's regular troops tried to make a stand, but the burghers of Ghent came upon them so furiously that they too became panic-stricken and fled. The Count himself ran with all his might, and as soon as he entered the city he ordered the gates to be shut. He was so anxious to save himself from the fury of Van Artevelde's soldiers that he wanted to close the gates at once and leave those of his own people who were still outside to their fate. But it was already too late. Van Artevelde's column had followed the retreating crowd so fast that it had already pushed its head into the town, and there was no driving it back. The five thousand "troublesome burghers," with their swords in their hands, and still crying "Ghent!" swarmed into Bruges, and quickly took possession of the town. The Count's army was utterly routed and scattered, and the Count himself would have been taken prisoner if one of the Ghent burghers had not hidden him and helped him to escape from the city.

Van Artevelde's soldiers, who had eaten the last of their food that morning in the belief that they would never eat another meal on earth, supped that night on the richest dishes that Bruges could supply; and now that the Count was overthrown, great wagon trains of provisions poured into poor, starving Ghent.

There was a great golden dragon on the belfry of Bruges, of which the Bruges people were very proud. That dragon had once stood on the Church of St. Sophia in Constantinople, and the Emperor Baldwin had sent it as a present to Bruges. In token of their victory Van Artevelde's "troublesome burghers" took down the golden dragon and carried it to Ghent.

THE DEFENCE OF ROCHELLE.

HOW THE CITY OF REFUGE FOUGHT FOR LIBERTY.

In the old times, when people were in the habit of fighting each other about their religion, the little French seaport Rochelle was called "the city of refuge." The Huguenots, or French Protestants, held the place, and when the armies of the French king tried to take it, in the latter part of the sixteenth century, they were beaten off and so badly used in the fight that the king was glad to make terms with the townspeople.

An agreement was therefore made that they should have their own religion, and manage their own affairs; and to make sure of this the king gave Rochelle so many special rights that it became almost a free city. After that, whenever a Protestant in any part of France found that he could not live peaceably in his own home, he went to Rochelle, and that is the way the place came to be called the city of refuge.

For a good many years the people of Rochelle went on living quietly. They had a fine harbor of their own, their trade was good, and they were allowed to manage their own affairs. At last the new King of France made up his mind that he would not have two religions in his country, but would make everybody believe as he did. This troubled the people of Rochelle, but the king sent them word that he only meant to make them change their religion by showing them that his was better, and that he did not intend to trouble them in any way.

In those days promises of that kind did not count for much; but the king's prime-minister, Cardinal Richelieu, who really managed everything, knew very well that Rochelle could give a great deal of trouble if it chose, and so, perhaps, he really would have let the town alone if it had not been for the meddling of the English prime-minister, Buckingham.

This Buckingham, with an English fleet and army, sailed into the harbor of Rochelle in the middle of July, 1627, and undertook to help the people against the French king. If Buckingham had been either a soldier or a sailor, he might have made himself master of the French king's forts near Rochelle at once; but, although he had command of a fleet and an army, he really knew nothing about the business of a commander, and he blundered so badly that the generals of the French king got fresh troops and provisions into the forts, and were able to hold them in spite of all that the English could do.

Seeing how matters stood, Richelieu at once sent an army to surround Rochelle, and at daylight on the 10th of August the people found a strong force in front of the town. Rochelle had not made up its mind to join the English, and the magistrates sent word to the French general that they wanted peace. They said they were loyal to the French king, and even offered to help drive the English away, if their king would promise not to break the treaty that had been made with them many years before.

It was too late to settle the matter in that way, however. The French general meant to make the town surrender, and so, while the English were fighting to get control of the island of Rhé, at some distance from the town, he began to build works around Rochelle. His plan was to shut the people up in the city and cut off their supplies of food; and when the Rochelle folk saw what he was doing, they opened fire on his men.

The war was now begun, and the Huguenots made terms with Buckingham, hoping, with his help, to win in the struggle. Buckingham promised to help them, and he did try to do so in his blundering way; but he did them more harm than good, for when he found that he could not take the forts he sailed away, taking with him three hundred tons of grain, which he ought to have sent into the town.

It was November when the English left, and Rochelle was in a very bad situation. Richelieu set to work to shut the town in and seal it up. He built strong works all around the land side, and then, with great labor, brought earth and stones and built a mole, or strip of land, nearly all the way across the mouth of the harbor, so that no boats could pass in or out.

RICHELIEU SURVEYING THE WORKS AT ROCHELLE.

The situation was a terrible one, but the people of Rochelle were brave, and had no thought of flinching. They chose the mayor, Guiton, for their commander, and when he accepted the office he laid his dagger on the table, saying: "I will thrust that dagger into the heart of the first man who speaks of giving up the town." He then went to work to defend the place. He strengthened the works, and made soldiers of all the men in the city, and all the boys, too, for that matter. Everybody who could handle a weapon of any kind had to take his place in the ranks. England had promised to send help, and the only question, Guiton thought, was whether or not he could hold out till the help should come; so he laid his plans to resist as long as possible.

The French in great numbers stormed the defences time after time; but the brave Rochellese always drove them back with great loss. It was clear from the first that Guiton would not give way, and that no column, however strong, could force the city gates. But there was an enemy inside the town which was harder to fight than the one outside. There was famine in Rochelle! The cattle were eaten up, and the horses went next. Then everything that could be turned into food was carefully used and made to go as far as it would. Guiton stopped every kind of waste; but day by day the food supply grew smaller, and the people grew weaker from hunger. Starvation was doing its work. Every day the list of deaths grew longer, and when people met in the streets they stared at each other with lean, white, hungry faces, wondering who would be the next to go.

Still these heroic people had no thought of giving up. They were fighting for liberty, and they loved that more than life. The French were daily charging their works, but could not move the stubborn, starving Rochellese.

The winter dragged on slowly. Spring came, and yet no help had come from England. In March the French, thinking that the people must be worn out, hurled their heaviest columns against the lines; but, do what they would, they could not break through anywhere, and had to go back to their works, and wait for famine to conquer a people who could not be conquered by arms.

One morning in May an English fleet was seen outside the mole. The news ran through the town like wildfire. Help was at hand, and the poor starving people were wild with joy. Men ran through the streets shouting and singing songs of thanksgiving. They had borne terrible sufferings, but now help was coming, and they were sure that their heroic endurance would not be thrown away. Thousands of their comrades had fallen fighting, and thousands of their women and children had starved to death; but what was that if, after all, Rochelle was not to lose her liberties?

Alas! their hope was a vain one, and their joy soon turned to sorrow. The English fleet did nothing. It hardly tried to do anything; but after lying within sight of the town for a while it sailed away again and left Rochelle to its fate.

Richelieu was sure that Guiton would surrender now, and so he sent a messenger to say that he would spare the lives of all the people if the town were given up within three days. But the gallant Guiton was not ready even yet to give up the struggle. "Tell Cardinal Richelieu," he said to the messenger, "that we are his very obedient servants;" and that was all the answer he had to make.

When the summer came some food was grown in the city gardens, but this went a very little way among so many people, and the famine had now grown frightful. The people gathered all the shellfish they could find at low tide. They ate the leaves off the trees, and even the grass of the gardens and lawns was used for food. Everything that could in any way help to support life was consumed; everything that could be boiled into the thinnest soup was turned to account; everything that could be chewed for its juice was used to quiet the pains of fierce hunger; but all was not enough. Men, women, and children died by thousands. Every morning when the new guard went to take the place of the old one many of the sentinels were found dead at their posts from starvation.

Still the heroic Guiton kept up the fight, and nobody dared say anything to him about giving up. He still hoped for help from England, and meant to hold out until it should come, cost what it might. In order that the soldiers might have a little more to eat, and live and fight a little longer, he turned all the old people and those who were too weak to fight out of the town. The French would not let these poor wretches pass their lines, but made an attack on them, and drove them back towards Rochelle. But Guiton would not open the city gates to them. He said they would starve to death if he let them into Rochelle, and they might as well die outside as inside the gates.

At last news came that the English had made a treaty with the French, and so there was no longer any hope of help for Rochelle, and truly the place could hold out no longer. The famine was at its worst. Out of about thirty thousand people only five thousand were left alive, and they were starving; of six hundred Englishmen who had stayed to help the Rochellese all were dead but sixty-two. Corpses lay thick in the streets, for the people were too weak, from fasting, even to bury their dead. The end had come. On the 30th of October, 1628, after nearly fifteen months of heroic effort and frightful suffering, Rochelle surrendered.

Richelieu at once sent food into the town, and treated the people very kindly; but he took away all the old rights and privileges of the city. He pulled down all the earth-works used by the defenders of the place, and gave orders that nobody should build even a garden fence anywhere near the town. He made a law that no Protestant who was not already a citizen of Rochelle should go thither to live, and that the "city of refuge" should never again receive any stranger without a permit from the king.

THE SAD STORY OF A BOY KING.

London took a holiday on the 16th of July, 1377. There were processions of merry-makers in the streets, and the windows were crowded with gayly dressed men, women, and children. The great lords, glittering in armor, and mounted upon splendid steel-clad horses, marched through the town. The bishops and clergymen in gorgeous robes made a more solemn, but not less attractive show. The trade-guilds were out in their best clothing, bearing the tools of their trades instead of arms. Clowns in motley, merry-makers of all kinds, great city dignitaries, lords and commons—everybody, in short, made a mad and merry holiday; and at night the houses were illuminated, and great bonfires were lighted in the streets.

All England was wild with joy; but the happiest person in the land was Richard Plantagenet, a boy eleven years of age. Indeed, it was for this boy's sake and in his honor that all this feasting and merry-making went on, for on that day young Richard was crowned King of England; and in those times a king of England was a much more important person than now, because the people had not then learned to govern themselves, and the king had powers which Englishmen would not allow any man to have in our time.

Richard was too young to govern wisely, and so a council was appointed to help him until he should grow up; but in the meantime he was a real king, boy as he was, and it is safe to say that he was the happiest boy in England on that July day, when all London took a holiday in his honor.

But if he had known what this crowning was to lead to, young Richard might have been very glad to change places with any baker's or butcher's boy in London. The boy king had some uncles and cousins who were very great people, and who gave him no little trouble after a while. He had wars on his hands, too, and needed a great deal more money than the people were willing to give him; and so, when he grew older and took the government into his own hands, he found troubles all around him. The Irish people rebelled frequently; the Scotch were hostile; there was trouble with Spain because Richard's uncle wanted to become king of that country, and there was a standing war with France.

But this was not all. In order to carry on these wars the king was obliged to have money; and when he ordered taxes to be collected the common people, led by Wat Tyler, rose in rebellion. They marched into London, seized the Tower, and put to death the treasurer of the kingdom, the Archbishop of Canterbury, and many other persons high in the government. Tyler was so insolent one day that the Lord Mayor of London killed him; but the boy king, who was only sixteen years old, seeing that the rebels were too strong for him, put himself at their head, and marched with them out of the city; and so the king, against whom the rebellion was made, became the leader of the rebels. As soon as matters grew quiet, however, he broke all the promises he had made, and punished the chief rebels very harshly.

Not long after this one of the king's uncles made himself master of the kingdom by force, and it was several years before Richard could put him out of power.

But the greatest of all Richard's troubles were yet to come. His cousin, Henry Bolingbroke, the son of old John of Gaunt, had misbehaved, and Richard had sent him out of England, not to return for ten years. But while Richard was in Ireland putting down a rebellion there, Henry came back to England, raised an army, and was joined by many of the most powerful men in the kingdom. When Richard came back from Ireland Henry made him a prisoner, and not long afterwards the great men made up their minds to set up Henry as the king instead of Richard. They made Richard sign a paper giving up his right to the crown, and then, to make the matter sure, Parliament passed a law that Richard should be king no longer.

Richard was only thirty-three years old when all this was done, but after so many troubles he might well have been glad to give up his kingship, if that had been the end of the matter. But a king who has been set aside is always a dangerous man to have in the kingdom, and it would not do to let Richard go free. He might gather his friends around him and give trouble. So it was decided that the unfortunate man should be shut up in a prison for the rest of his life.

But even this was not the worst of the matter. Richard had a wife—Queen Isabella—whom he loved very dearly, and if the two could have gone away together into some quiet place to live, they might still have been happy in spite of being under guard all the time. But the new king would not have it so. He gave orders that Richard should be shut up closely in a prison, and that Isabella should go back to France, where Richard had married her.

This was a terrible thing for the young man and his younger wife, who might have had a long life of happiness still before them if Richard had never been a king. But Richard had been King of England, and so he had to give up both his freedom and his wife.

In his play of "King Richard the Second" Shakespeare makes a very touching scene of their parting. In the play their farewell takes place in the street, as shown in our picture. Isabella, anxious to see her husband once more before they part forever, waits at a point which she knows he must pass on his way to prison. There they meet and talk together for the last time on earth. The words which Shakespeare puts into their mouths are terribly sad, but very beautiful. You will find the scene at the beginning of Act V. of the play. The picture shows the two at the moment when Richard moves away to his prison, leaving Isabella to mourn for him in a nunnery for the rest of her life.

It is not certainly known what became of Richard after he was taken to prison. It is believed that he was murdered there—perhaps starved to death—but there is a story that he got away and lived in Scotland, dying there in 1419. It is not at all likely that the story is true, however, and the common belief has always been that he died or was killed in Pontefract Castle, where he was imprisoned.

THE PARTING BETWEEN KING RICHARD II. AND QUEEN ISABELLA.

However that may be, Richard's life was a terribly unhappy one, and all his sorrows grew out of the fact that he was a king. If he could have looked forward on that July day when the people were making merry in his honor, and could have known all that was to happen to him, instead of being the happiest boy in England on his coronation day, he would have been the most wretched.

TWO OBSCURE HEROES.

HOW THE PARTISAN WARFARE IN THE CAROLINAS WAS BEGUN.

When the British marched up from Savannah and took Charleston, in the spring of 1780, they thought the Revolution was at an end in the Southern States, and it really seemed so. Even the patriots thought it was useless to resist any longer, and so when the British ordered all the people to come together at different places and enrol themselves as British subjects, most of them were ready to do it, simply because they thought they could not help themselves.

Only a few daring men here and there were bold enough to think of refusing, and but for them the British could have set up the royal power again in South Carolina, and then they would have been free to take their whole force against the patriots farther north. The fate of the whole country depended, to a large extent, upon the courage of the few men who would not give up even at such a time, but kept up the fight against all odds. These brave men forced the British to keep an army in the South which they needed farther north.

The credit of beginning this kind of partisan warfare belongs chiefly to two or three plain men, who did it simply because they loved their country more than their ease.

The man who first began it was Justice Gaston—a white-haired patriot who lived on a little stream called Fishing Creek, near Rocky Mount. He was eighty years of age, and might well have thought himself too old to care about war matters; but he was a brave man and a patriot, and the people who lived near him were in the habit of taking his advice and doing as he did.

When the news came that Tarleton had killed a band of patriots under Colonel Buford in cold blood Justice Gaston called his nine sons and many of his nephews around him. Joining hands, these young men promised each other that they never would take the British oath, and never would give up the cause, come what might.

Soon afterwards a British force came to the neighborhood, and all the people were ordered to meet at Rocky Mount to enrol their names and take the oath. One of the British officers went to see Justice Gaston, and tried to persuade him that it was folly to refuse. He knew that if Gaston advised the people to give up, there would be no trouble; but the white-haired patriot told him to his face that he would never take the oath himself or advise anybody else to do so.

As soon as the officer left the old man sent for his friends, and about thirty brave fellows met at his house that night, with their rifles in their hands. They knew there would be a strong force of British and Tories at Rocky Mount the next day, but, in spite of the odds against them, they made up their minds to attack the place, and when the time came they did so. Creeping through the woods, they suddenly came upon the crowd, and after a sharp fight sent the British flying helter-skelter in every direction. This stopped the work of enrolling the people as British subjects, and it did more than that. It showed the patriots through the whole country that they could still give the British a great deal of trouble, and after this affair many of the men who had thought of giving up rubbed up their rifles instead, and formed little bands of fighting men to keep the war going.

Another man who did much to stir up partisan warfare was the Rev. William Martin, an old and pious preacher in the Scotch-Irish settlements. These Scotch-Irish were very religious people, and their preacher was their leader in all things. One Sunday, after the news had come to the settlement that Buford's men had been killed by the British in cold blood, the eloquent old man went into his pulpit and preached about the duty of fighting. In the afternoon he preached again, and even when the service was over he went on in the open air, still preaching to the people how they should fight for their country, until all the men in the settlement were full of fighting spirit. The women told the men to go and do their duty, and that they would take care of the crops.

These little bands of patriots were too small to fight regular battles, or even to hold strong posts. They had to hide in the woods and swamps, and only came out when they saw a chance to strike a blow. Then the blow fell like lightning, and the men who dealt it quickly hid themselves again.

They had signs by which they told each other what they were going to do. A twig bent down, a few stones strung along a path, or any other of a hundred small signs, served to tell every patriot when and where to meet his friends. A man riding about, breaking a twig here and there, or making some other sign of the kind, could call together a large force at a chosen spot within a few hours. The men brought out in this way would fall suddenly upon some stray British force that was off its guard, and utterly destroy it. The British would at once send a strong body of troops to punish the daring patriots, but the redcoat leader would look in vain for anybody to punish. The patriots could scatter and hide as quickly as they could come together.

MARTIN PREACHING TO THE PEOPLE ON THE DUTY OF FIGHTING.

Finding that they could not destroy these patriot companies, the British and Tories took their revenge on women and children. They burned the houses of the patriots, carried off their crops, and killed their cattle, so as to starve their families; but the women were as brave us the men, and from first to last not one of them ever wished her husband or son to give up the fight.

If the patriots could not conquer the British, they at least kept them in a hornets' nest. If they could not drive them out of South Carolina, they could keep them there, which was nearly as good a thing to do, because every soldier that Cornwallis had to keep in the South would have been sent to some other part of the country to fight the Americans if the Carolinians had let the British alone.

In this way small bands of resolute men kept Cornwallis busy, and held the state for the American cause, until General Greene went south and took command. Greene was one of the greatest of the American generals, and after a long campaign he drove the British out of the state. But if it had not been for the partisans the South would have been lost long before he could be spared to go there; and if the partisans had not kept a British army busy there, it might have gone very hard with the Americans in the rest of the country.

When we rejoice in the freedom of our country we ought not to forget how much we owe the partisans, and especially such men as Justice Gaston and the Rev. William Martin, who first set the partisans at their work. It would have been much easier and pleasanter for them to remain quiet under British rule; and they had nothing to gain for themselves, but everything to lose, by the course they took. Gaston knew that his home would be burned for what he did, and the eloquent old Scotch preacher knew that he would be put into a prison-pen for preaching war sermons to his people; but they were not men to flinch. They cared more for their country than for themselves, and it was precisely that kind of men throughout the land, from New England to Georgia, who won liberty for us by seven years of hard fighting and terrible suffering.

THE CHARGE OF THE HOUNDS.

AN INCIDENT OF THE CREEK WAR.

A terrible bit of news was carried from mouth to mouth through the region that is now Alabama at the beginning of September, 1813. The country was at that time in the midst of the second war with Great Britain, and for a long time British agents had been trying to persuade the Creeks—a powerful nation of half-civilized but very warlike Indians who lived in Alabama—to join in the war and destroy the white settlements in the Southwest.

For some time the Creeks hesitated, and it was uncertain what they would do. But during the summer of 1813 they broke out in hostility, and on the 30th of August their great leader, Weatherford, or the Red Eagle, as they called him, stormed Fort Mims, the strongest fort in the Southwest. He took the fort by surprise, with a thousand warriors behind him, and, after five hours of terrible fighting, destroyed it, killing about five hundred men, women, and children.

This was the news that startled the settlers in the region where the Alabama and Tombigbee rivers come together. It was certain, after such a massacre as that, that the Indians meant to destroy the settlements, and kill all the white people without mercy.

In order to protect themselves and their families the settlers built rude forts by setting pieces of timber endwise in the ground, and the people hurried to these places for safety. Leaving their homes to be burned, their crops to be destroyed, and their cattle to be killed or carried off by the Indians, the settlers hastily got together what food they could, and took their families into the nearest forts.

One of the smallest of these stockade forts was called Sinquefield. It stood in what is now Clarke County, Alabama, and, as that region was very thinly settled, there were not enough men to make a strong force for the defence of the fort. But the brave farmers and hunters thought they could hold the place, and so they took their families thither as quickly as they could.

Two families, numbering seventeen persons, found it was not easy to go to Sinquefield on the 2d of September, and so, as they were pretty sure that there were no Indians in their neighborhood as yet, they made up their minds to stay one more night at a house a few miles from the fort. That night they were attacked, and all but five of them were killed. Those who got away carried the news of what had happened to the fort, and a party was sent out to bring in the bodies.

The next day all the people in Fort Sinquefield went out to bury their dead friends in a valley at some little distance from the fort, and, strange as it seems, they took no arms with them. Believing that there were no Indians near the place, they left the gates of the fortress open, and went out in a body without their guns.

As a matter of fact there was a large body of Indians not only very near them, but actually looking at them all the time. The celebrated Prophet Francis was in command, and in his sly way he had crept as near the fort as possible to look for a good chance to attack it. Making his men lie down and crawl like snakes, he had reached a point only a few hundred yards from the stockade without alarming the people, and now, while they stood around the graves of their friends without arms to defend themselves with, a host of their savage enemies lay looking at them from the grass and bushes on the hill.

As soon as he saw that the right moment had come, Francis sprang up with a savage war-cry, and at the head of his warriors made a dash at the gates. He had seen that the men outside were unarmed, and his plan was to get to the gates before they could reach them, and thus get all the people of the place at his mercy in an open field and without arms to fight with.

The fort people were quick to see what his purpose was, and the men hurried forward with all their might, hoping to reach the fort before the savages could get there. By running at the top of their speed they did this, and closed the gates in time to keep the Indians out. But, to their horror, they then saw that their wives and children were shut out too. Unable to run so fast as the men had done, the women and children had fallen behind, and now the Indians were between them and the gates!

Seeing that he had missed his chance of getting possession of the fort, Francis turned upon the women and children with savage delight in the thought of butchering these helpless creatures in the sight of their husbands, fathers, and brothers.

It was a moment of terror. There were not half enough white men in the fort to master so large a force of Indians, and if there had been it was easy to see that by the time they could get their rifles and go to the rescue it would be too late.

At that moment the hero of this bit of history came upon the scene. This was a young man named Isaac Haden. He was a notable huntsman, who kept a famous pack of hounds—fierce brutes, thoroughly trained to run down and seize any live thing that their master chose to chase. This young man had been out in search of stray cattle, and just at the moment when matters were at their worst he rode up to the fort, followed by his sixty dogs.

Isaac Haden had a cool head and a very daring spirit. He was in the habit of taking in a situation at a glance, deciding quickly what was to be done, and then doing it at any risk that might be necessary. As soon as he saw how the women and children were placed, he cried out to his dogs, and, at the head of the bellowing pack, charged upon the flank of the Indians. The dogs did their work with a spirit equal to their master's. For each to seize a red warrior and drag him to earth was the work of a moment, and the whole body of savages was soon in confusion. For a time they had all they could do to defend themselves against the unlooked-for assault of the fierce animals, and before they could beat off the dogs the men of the fort came out and joined in the attack, so that the women and children had time to make their way inside the gates, only one of them, a Mrs. Phillips, having been killed.

The men, of course, had to follow the women closely, as they were much too weak in numbers to risk a battle outside. If they had done so the Indians would have overcome them quickly, and then the fort and everybody in it would have been at their mercy, so the settlers hurried into the fort as soon as the women were safe.

But the hero who had saved the people by his quickness and courage was left outside, and not only so, but the savages were between him and the fort. He had charged entirely through the war party, and was now beyond their line, alone, and with no chance of help from any quarter.

His hope of saving himself was very small indeed; but he had saved all those helpless women and little children, and he was a brave enough fellow to die willingly for such a purpose as that if he must. But brave men do not give up easily, and young Haden did not mean to die without a last effort to save himself.

"JUST AT THE MOMENT WHEN MATTERS WERE AT THEIR WORST, HE RODE UP."

Blowing a loud blast upon his hunting-horn to call his remaining dogs around him, he drew his pistols—one in each hand—and plunged spurs into his horse's flanks. In spite of the numbers against him he broke through the mass of savages, but the gallant horse that bore him fell dead as he cleared the Indian ranks. Haden had fired both his pistols, and had no time to load them again. He was practically unarmed now, and the distance he still had to go before reaching the gates was considerable. His chance of escape seemed smaller than ever, but he quickly sprang from the saddle, and ran with all his might, hotly pursued, and under a terrific fire from the rifles of the savages. The gate was held a little way open for him to pass, and when he entered the fort his nearest pursuers were so close at his heels that there was barely time for the men to shut the gate in their faces.

Strangely enough, the brave young fellow was not hurt in any way. Five bullets had passed through his clothes, but his skin was not broken.

THE STORY OF A WINTER CAMPAIGN.

Nearly all the countries in Europe were making war upon France in 1795. The French people had set up a republic, and all the kingdoms round about were trying to make them submit to a king again. This had been going on for several years, and sometimes it looked as though the French would be beaten, in spite of their brave struggles to keep their enemies back and manage their own affairs in their own way.

At one time everything went against the French. Their armies were worn out with fighting, their supply of guns had run short, they had no powder, and their money matters were in so bad a state that it seemed hardly possible for France to hold out any longer. In the meantime England, Austria, Spain, Holland, Piedmont, and Prussia, besides many of the small German states, had joined together to fight France, and their armies were on every side of her.

A country in such a state as that, with so many powerful enemies on every side, might well have given up; but the French are a brave people, and they were fighting for their liberties. Instead of giving up in despair, they set to work with all their might to carry on the war.

The first thing to be done was to raise new armies, and so they called for men, and the men came forward in great numbers from every part of the country. In a little while they had more men to make soldiers of than had ever before been brought together in France. But this was only a beginning. The men were not yet trained soldiers, and even if they had been, they had no guns and no powder; no clothing was to be had, and there was very little food for them to eat. Still the French did not despair.

Knowing that there would not be time enough to train the new men, they put some of their old soldiers in each regiment of new ones, so that the new men might learn from the veterans how to march and how to fight.

In the meantime they had set up armories, and were making guns as fast as they could. Their greatest trouble was about powder. They had chemists who knew how to make it, but they had no nitre to make it of, and did not know at first how to get any. At last one of their chemists said that there was some nitre—from a few ounces to a pound or two—in the earth of every cellar floor; and that if all the nitre in all the cellar floors of France could be collected, it would be enough to make plenty of powder.

But how to get this nitre was a question. The cellar floors must be dug up, the earth must be washed, and the water must be carefully passed through a course of chemical treatment in order to get the nitre, free from earth and from all other things with which it was mixed. It would take many days for a chemist to extract the nitre from the earth of a singly cellar, and then he would get only a pound or two of it at most.

It did not seem likely that much could be done in this way, but all the people were anxious to help, and so the cry went up from every part of the country, "Send us chemists to teach us how, and we will do the work and get the nitre ourselves." This was quickly done. All the chemists were set at work teaching the people how to get a little nitre out of a great deal of earth, and then every family went to work. In a little while the nitre began to come in to the powder-factories. Each family sent its little parcel of the precious salt as a free gift to the country. Some of them were so proud and glad of the chance to help that they dressed their little packages of nitre in ribbons of the national colors, and wrote patriotic words upon them. Each little parcel held only a few ounces, or at most a pound or two, of the white salt; but the parcels came in by tens of thousands, and in a few weeks there were hundreds of tons of nitre at the powder-mills.

As soon as there was powder enough the new armies began to press their enemies, and, during the summer and fall of 1794, they steadily drove them back. When they met their foes in battle they nearly always forced them to give way. They charged upon forts and took them at the point of the bayonet; cities and towns everywhere fell into their hands, and by the time that winter set in they were so used to winning battles that nothing seemed too hard for them to undertake.

But the French soldiers were in a very bad condition to stand the cold of winter. One great army, under General Pichegru, which had driven the English and Dutch far into the Netherlands, was really almost naked. The shoes of the soldiers were worn out, and so they had to wrap their feet in wisps of straw to keep them from freezing. Many of the men had not clothing enough to cover their nakedness, and, for decency's sake, had to plait straw into mats which they wore around their shoulders like blankets. They had no tents to sleep in, but, nearly naked as they were, had to lie down in the snow or on the hard frozen ground, and sleep as well as they could in the bitter winter weather.

There never was an army more in need of a good rest in winter-quarters, and as two great rivers lay in front of them, it seemed impossible to do anything more until spring. The English and Dutch were already safely housed for the winter, feeling perfectly sure that the French could not cross the rivers or march in any direction until the beginning of the next summer.

The French generals, therefore, put their men into the best quarters they could get for them, and the poor, half-naked, barefooted soldiers were glad to think that their work for that year was done.

Day by day the weather grew colder. The ground was frozen hard, and ice began running in the rivers. After a little while the floating ice became so thick that the rivers were choked with it. When Christmas came the stream nearest the French was frozen over, and three days later the ice was so hard that the surface of the river was as firm as the solid ground.

Then came an order from General Pichegru to shoulder arms and march. In the bitterest weather of that terrible winter the barefooted, half-clad French soldiers left their huts, and marched against their foes. Crossing the first river on the ice, they fell upon the surprised Dutch and utterly routed them. About the same time they made a dash at the strong fortified posts along the river, and captured them.

The French were now masters of the large island that lay between the two rivers, for they are really only two branches of one river, and the land between them is an island. But the ice in the farther stream was not yet hard enough to bear the weight of cannon, so Pichegru had to stay where he was for a time. Both sides now watched the weather, the French hoping for still harder frosts, while their enemies prayed for a thaw.

The cold weather continued, and day by day the ice became firmer. On the 8th of January, 1795, Pichegru began to cross, and on the 10th his whole army had passed the stream, while his enemies were rapidly retreating. He pushed forward into the country, sending his columns in different directions to press the enemy at every point. The barefooted, half-naked French soldiers were full of spirit, and in spite of frost and snow and rough frozen roads they marched steadily and rapidly. City after city fell before them, and on the 20th of January they marched into Amsterdam itself, and were complete conquerors.

Hungry and half-frozen as they were, it would not have been strange if these poor soldiers had rushed into the warm houses of the city and helped themselves to food and clothing. But they did nothing of the kind. They stacked their arms in the streets and public squares, and quietly waited in the snow, patiently bearing the bitter cold of the wind for several hours, while the magistrates were getting houses and food and clothing ready for them.

This whole campaign was wonderful, and on almost every day some strange thing happened; but, perhaps, the strangest of all the events in this winter war was that which is shown in the picture. Pichegru, learning that there was a fleet of the enemy's vessels lying at anchor near the island of Texel, sent a column of cavalry, with some cannon, in that direction, to see if anything could be done. The cavalry found the Zuyder Zee hard frozen, and the ships firmly locked in the ice. So they put spurs to their horses, galloped over the frozen surface of the sea, marched up to the ships, and called on them to surrender. It was a new thing in war for ships to be charged by men on horseback; but there the horsemen were, with strong ice under them, and the ships could not sail away from them. The sailors could make a fight, of course, but the cavalry, with their cannon, were too strong for them, and so they surrendered without a battle, and for the first time in history a body of hussars captured a squadron of ships at anchor.

CAPTURE OF THE DUTCH FLEET BY THE SOLDIERS OF THE FRENCH REPUBLIC.

YOUNG WASHINGTON IN THE WOODS.

THE STORY OF A PERILOUS JOURNEY.

No man ever lived whose name is more honored than that of George Washington, and no man ever deserved his fame more. All the success that ever came to him was won by hard work. He succeeded because he was the kind of man that he was, and not in the least because he had "a good chance" to distinguish himself. He never owed anything to "good luck," nor even to a special education in the business of a soldier. Some men are called great because they have succeeded in doing great things; but he succeeded in doing great things because he was great in himself.

Everybody who knew him, even as a boy, seems to have respected as well as liked him. There was something in his character which made men think well of him. When he was only sixteen years of age Lord Fairfax admired him to such a degree that he appointed him to a post which not many men would have been trusted to fill. He put the boy at the head of a surveying party, and sent him across the mountains to survey the valley of Virginia—a vast region which was then unsettled. So well did Washington perform this difficult and dangerous task that a few years later, when he was only twenty-one years old, the Governor of Virginia picked him out for a more delicate and dangerous piece of work.

The English colonies lay along the Atlantic coast, while the French held Canada. The country west of the Alleghany Mountains, which we now know as Ohio, Indiana, Illinois, etc., was claimed by both the French and the English, though only the Indians lived there. The French made friends of the savages, and began building forts at different points in that region, and putting soldiers there to keep the English away. The Governor of Virginia wanted to put a stop to this, and so he resolved to send a messenger into "the Great Woods," as the western country was called, to warn the French off, and to win the friendship of the Indians if possible.

For such a service he needed a man with a cool head, good sense, great courage, and, above all, what boys call "grit;" for whoever should go would have to make his way for many hundreds of miles through a trackless wilderness, over mountains and rivers, and among hostile Indians. Young Washington had already shown what stuff he was made of, and, young as he was, he was regarded as a remarkable man. The governor therefore picked him out as the very best person for the work that was to be done.

It was November when Washington set out, and the weather was very cold and wet. He took four white men and two Indians with him, the white men being hunters who knew how to live in the woods. As the country they had to pass through was a wilderness, they had to carry all their supplies with them on pack-horses. They rode all day through the woods, and when night came slept in little tents by some spring or watercourse. Day after day they marched forward, until at last they reached an Indian village, near the spot where Pittsburgh now stands, and there they halted to make friends with the Indians.

This was not very easy, as the French had already had a good deal to do with the tribes in that region; but Washington persuaded the chief, whose name was Tanacharisson, to go with him to visit the French commander, who was stationed in a fort hundreds of miles away, near Lake Erie.

This march, like the other, was slow and full of hardships; but at last the fort was reached, and Washington delivered his message to the French officer. A day or two later the Frenchman gave him his answer, which was that the western country belonged to the French, and that they had no notion of giving it up.

All the trouble Washington had met in going north was nothing compared with what was before him in going back to Virginia again. The winter was now at its worst, and the weather was terrible. The rivers and creeks were full of floating ice, and the woods were banked high with snow. But Washington was not to be daunted by any kind of difficulty. He set out on his return march, and with the aid of canoes, in which his baggage was carried down a small stream that ran in that direction, he took his party as far as Venango, in the northwestern part of Pennsylvania.

There he found that he could go no farther on horseback. The ground was frozen on top, but soft beneath, and the poor horses broke through the hard crust at every step. There was a French fort at Venango, and Washington might have waited there very comfortably for better weather; but it was his duty to get back to Virginia as soon as possible with the French commander's answer, and so he made up his mind to go on, even at the risk of his life.

Leaving the rest of the party to come when they could with the horses, Washington and a single companion named Gist set out on foot for the long winter march. As they had no pack-horses to carry tents and cooking-vessels and food, they had to leave everything behind except what they could carry on their backs; and as they were obliged to take their rifles, powder-horns, and bullet-pouches, their hunting-knives and hatchets, and a blanket apiece, they were pretty heavily loaded, and could not afford to burden themselves with much else.

Day by day the two brave fellows trudged on through the snow-drifts, sleeping at night as best they could, exposed to the biting cold of the winter, without shelter, except such as the woods afforded. There were other dangers besides cold and hunger. At one time a treacherous Indian, who had offered to act as guide, tried to lead the two white men into a trap. As they suspected his purpose, they refused to do as he wished, and a little later he suddenly turned about and shot at Washington, who was only a few paces distant. Missing his aim, he was quickly overpowered, and Gist wanted to kill him, not merely because he deserved to be put to death for his treachery, but also because, if allowed to go free, he was pretty sure to bring other hostile Indians to attack the lonely travellers during the night.

WASHINGTON AS A SURVEYOR.

But Washington would not have him killed. He made him build a camp-fire, and then told him to leave them at once. The Indian did so, and as soon as it was certain that he was out of sight and hearing the two young men set out to make their escape. They knew the Indian would soon come back with others, and that their only chance for life was to push on as fast as they could. The Indians could track them in the snow, but by setting out at once they hoped to get so far ahead that they could not be easily overtaken.

It was already night, and the travellers were weary from their day's march, but they could not afford to stop or rest. All through the night they toiled on. Morning came, and they must have felt it nearly impossible to drag their weary feet farther, but still they made no halt. On and on they went, and it was not till night came again that they thought it safe at last to stop for the rest and sleep they needed so badly. The strain they had undergone must have been fearful. They were already weary and wayworn when they first met the treacherous Indian, and after that they had toiled through the snow for two days and a night without stopping to rest or daring to refresh themselves with sleep.

Just before reaching their journey's end they arrived at the brink of a river which they expected to find frozen over; but they found it full of floating ice instead. Without boat or bridge, there seemed no chance of getting across; but after a while they managed to make a rude raft, and upon this they undertook to push themselves across with long poles.

The current was very strong, the raft was hard to manage, and the great fields of ice forced it out of its course. In trying to push it in the right direction, Washington missed his footing and fell into the icy river. His situation was very dangerous, but by a hard struggle he got upon the floating logs again. Still the current swept them along, and they could not reach either shore of the stream.

At last they managed to leap from the logs, not to the bank, but to a small island in the river. There they were very little better off than on the raft. They were on land, it is true, but there was still no way of getting to shore; and as there was nothing on the island to make a fire with, Washington was forced, drenched as he was with ice-water, to pass the long winter night in the open air, without so much as a tiny blaze or a handful of coals by which to warm himself.

Unfortunately the night proved to be a very cold one, and poor Gist's feet and hands were frozen before morning. Washington got no frost-bites, but his sufferings must have been great.

During the night that part of the stream which lay between the island and the shore that Washington wished to reach froze over, and in the morning the travellers were able to renew their journey. Once across that, the worst of their troubles were over.

Is it any wonder that a young man who did his duty in this way rapidly rose to distinction? He was always in earnest in his work, and always did it with all his might. He never shammed or shirked. He never let his own comfort or his own interest stand in the way when there was a duty to be done. He was a great man before he became a celebrated one, and the wisest men in the country found out the fact.

When the revolution came there were other soldiers older and better known than Washington, but there were men in Congress who had watched his career carefully. They made him, therefore, commander-in-chief of the American armies, knowing that nobody else was so sure to do the very best that could be done for the country. They did not make him a great man by appointing him to the chief command; they appointed him because they knew he was a great man already.

THE STORY OF CATHERINE.

Peter the Great, the emperor who, in a few years, changed Russia from a country of half-savage tribes into a great European nation, was one day visiting one of his officers, and saw in his house a young girl, who attracted his attention by her beauty and her graceful manners. This girl was a prisoner named Martha, and she was living as a sort of servant and housekeeper in the family of the Russian officer. She had been taken prisoner when the town she lived in was captured. Nobody knows, even to this day, exactly who she was, except that she was a poor orphan girl who had been brought up by a village clergyman; but it is generally believed that her father was a Livonian peasant.

Martha's beauty and the brightness of her mind pleased the emperor so much that, after a while, he made up his mind to marry her, in spite of her humble origin. Peter was in the habit of doing pretty much as he pleased, whether his nobles liked it or not; but even he dared not make a captive peasant girl the Empress of Russia. He therefore married her privately, in the presence of a few of his nearest friends, who were charged to keep the secret. Before the marriage took place he had Martha baptized in the Russian Church, and changed her name to Catherine.

Now Peter had a bad habit of losing his temper, and getting so angry that he fell into fits. As he was an absolute monarch and could do whatever he liked, it was very dangerous for anybody to go near him when he was angry. He could have a head chopped off as easily as he could order his breakfast. But he was very fond of Catherine, and she was the only person who was not in the least afraid of him. She soon learned how to manage him, and even in his worst fits she could soothe and quiet the old bear.

Peter was nearly always at war, and in spite of the hardships and dangers of the camp and battle-field Catherine always marched with him at the head of the army. The soldiers wondered at her bravery, and learned to like her more than anybody else. If food was scarce, the roads rough, and the marches long, they remembered, that Catherine was with them, and were ashamed to grumble. If she could stand the hardships and face the dangers, they thought rough soldiers ought not to complain.

Catherine was a wise woman as well as a brave one. She soon learned as much of the art of war as Peter knew, and in every time of doubt or difficulty her advice was asked, and her opinion counted for as much as if she had been one of the generals. After she had thus shown how able a woman she was, and had won the friendship of everybody about her by her good temper and her pleasant ways, Peter publicly announced his marriage, and declared Catherine to be his wife and czarina. But still he did not crown her.

This was in the year 1711, and immediately afterwards Peter marched into the Turkish country at the head of forty thousand men. This army was not nearly large enough to meet the Turks, but Peter had other armies in different places, and had ordered all of them to meet him on the march. For various reasons all these armies failed to join him, and he found himself in a Turkish province with a very small number of troops. The danger was so great that he ordered Catherine and all the other women to go back to a place of safety. But Catherine would not go. She had made up her mind to stay with Peter at the head of the army, and was so obstinate about it that at last Peter gave her leave to remain. Then the wives of the generals, and, finally, of the lower officers, wanted to stay also. She persuaded Peter to let them do so, and the end of it was that the women all stayed with the army.

Everything went against Peter on this march. The weather was very dry. Swarms of locusts were in the country, eating every green thing. There was no food for the horses, and many of them starved to death. It was hard for the Russians to go forward or to go backward, and harder still to stay where they were.

At last the soldiers in front reported that the Turks were coming, and Peter soon saw a great army of two hundred thousand fierce Moslems in front of his little force, which counted up only thirty-eight thousand men. Seeing the odds against him he gave the order to retreat, and the army began its backward march. As it neared the river Pruth a new danger showed itself. The advance-guard brought word that a great force of savage Crim Tartars held the other bank of the river, completely cutting off Peter's retreat.

The state of things seemed hopeless. With two hundred thousand Turks on one side, and a strong force of Crim Tartars holding a river on the other, Peter's little army was completely hemmed in. There was no water in the camp, and when the soldiers went to the river for it, the Tartars on the other shore kept up a fierce fight with them. A great horde of Turkish cavalry tried hard to cut off the supply entirely by pushing themselves between Peter's camp and the river, but the Russians managed to keep them back by hard fighting, and to keep a road open to the river.

Peter knew now that unless help should come to him in some shape, and that very quickly, he must lose not only his army, but his empire also, for if the Turks should take him prisoner, it was certain that his many enemies would soon conquer Russia, and divide the country among themselves. He saw no chance of help coming, but he made up his mind to fight as long as he could. He formed his men in a hollow square, with the women in the middle, and faced his enemies.

The Turks flung themselves in great masses upon his lines, trying to crush the little force of Russians by mere numbers. But Peter's brave men remembered that Catherine was inside their hollow square, and they stood firmly at their posts, driving back the Turks with frightful slaughter. Again and again and again they fell upon his lines in heavy masses, and again and again and again they were driven back, leaving the field black with their dead.

This could not go on forever, of course, and both sides saw what the end must be. As the Turks had many times more men than Peter, it was plain that they would, at last, win by destroying all the Russians.

For three days and nights the terrible slaughter went on. Peter's men beat back the Turks at every charge, but every hour their line grew thinner. At the end of the third day sixteen thousand of their brave comrades lay dead upon the field, and only twenty-two thousand remained to face the enemy.

Towards night on the third day a terrible rumor spread through their camp. A whisper ran along the line that *the ammunition was giving out*. A few more shots from each soldier's gun, and there would be nothing left to fight with.

Then Peter fell into the sulks. As long as he could fight he had kept up his spirits, but now that all was lost, and his great career seemed near its end, he grew angry, and went to his tent to have one of his savage fits. He gave orders that nobody should come near him, and there was no officer or soldier in all the army who would have dared enter the tent where he lay, in his dangerous mood.

But if Peter had given up in despair, Catherine had not. In spite of Peter's order and his anger, she boldly went into his tent, and asked him to give her leave to put an end to the war by making a treaty of peace with the Turks, if she could. It seemed absurd to talk of such a thing, or to expect the Turks to make peace on any terms when they had so good a chance to conquer Peter, once for all, and to make him their prisoner. Nobody but Catherine, perhaps, would have thought of such a thing; but Catherine was a woman born for great affairs, and she had no thought of giving up any chance there might be to save Peter and the empire.

Her first difficulty was with Peter himself. She could not offer terms of peace to the Turks until Peter gave her leave, and promised to fulfil whatever bargain she might make with them. She managed this part of the matter, and then set to work at the greater task of dealing with the Turks.

"SHE WENT BOLDLY INTO HIS TENT."

She knew that the Turkish army was under the command of the Grand Vizier, and she knew something of the ways of Grand Viziers. It was not worth while to send any kind of messenger to a Turkish commander without sending him also a bribe in the shape of a present, and Catherine was sure that the bribe must be a very large one to buy the peace she wanted. But where was she to get the present? There was no money in Peter's army-chest, and no way of getting any from Russia. Catherine was not discouraged by that fact. She first got together all her own jewels, and then went to all the officers' wives and asked each of them for whatever she had that was valuable—money, jewels, and plate. She gave each of them a receipt for what she took, and promised to pay them the value of their goods when she should get back to Moscow. She went in this way throughout the camp, and got together all the money, all the jewelry, and all the silver plate that were to be found in the army. No one person had much, of course; but when the things were collected together, they made a very rich present, or bribe, for the Grand Vizier.

With this for a beginning, Catherine soon convinced the Turkish commander that it was better to make peace with Russia than to run the risk of having to fight the great armies that were already marching towards Turkey. After some bargaining she secured a treaty which allowed Peter to go back to Russia in safety, and thus she saved the czar and the empire.

A few years later Peter crowned her as Empress of Russia, and when he died he named her as the fittest person to be his successor on the throne.

Thus the peasant girl of Livonia, who was made a captive in war and a servant, rose by her genius and courage to be the sole ruler of a great empire—the first woman who ever reigned over Russia. It is a strange but true story.

THE VIRGINIA WIFE-MARKET.

TWO SHIPLOADS OF SWEETHEARTS AND THE PRICES PAID FOR THEM.

The first English settlement in America that came to anything was made in the most absurd way possible. A great company of London merchants set about the work of planting an English colony in Virginia, and they were very much in earnest about it too; but if they had been as anxious to have the scheme fail as they were to make it succeed, they could hardly have done worse for it than they did in some respects.

They knew that the colonists must have something to eat and must defend themselves against the Indians, and so it ought to have been plain to them that the first men sent out must be stout farmers, who could cut down trees, plough the ground, raise food enough for the people to eat, and handle guns well, if need be. The work to be done was that of farmers, wood-choppers, and men who could make a living for themselves in a new country, and common-sense ought to have led the London Company to send out nobody but men of that kind to make the first settlement. Then, after those men had cleared some land, built some houses, and raised their first crop, men of other kinds might have been sent as fast as there was need for their services.

But that was not the way in which the London Company went to work. They chose for their first settlers about the most unfit men they could have found for such a purpose. There were one hundred and five of them in all, and forty-eight of them—or nearly half of the whole company—were what people in those days called "gentlemen"—that is to say, they were the sons of rich men. They had never learned how to do any kind of work, and had been brought up to think that a gentleman could not work without degrading himself and losing his right to be called a gentleman. There were a good many "servants" also in the party, and probably most of them were brought to wait upon the gentlemen. There were very few farmers and not many mechanics in the party, although farmers and mechanics were the men most needed. There were some goldsmiths, who expected to work the gold as soon as the colonists should find it, and there was a perfume-maker. It is hard to say in what way this perfume-man was expected to make himself useful in the work of planting a settlement in the swamps of Virginia; but, as there were so many fine "gentlemen" in the party, the perfumer probably thought his wares would be in demand.

None of the men brought families with them. They were single men, who came out to this country, not to make comfortable homes for wives and children, by hard and patient work, but to find gold and pearls, or to grow rich in some other quick and easy way, and then to go back and live in ease in England.

It is a wonder that such men ever succeeded in planting a settlement at all. From the first it does not seem to have been clear to them that they ought to raise plenty of food for themselves and learn how to live by their own work. They expected the company in London to send them most of their food and everything else that they needed. They had plenty of rich land and a good climate, but they expected to be fed by people three thousand miles away, across a great ocean.

Luckily, there was one man of sense and spirit among them—the celebrated Captain John Smith—who got them to work a little, and, after many hardships and two or three narrow escapes from failure, the colony was firmly planted.

The London Company sent out ships every year with supplies and fresh colonists; but, strange as it seems, most of the men sent were unmarried, and even those who had wives and children left them in England.

When we think of it, this was a very bad way to begin the work of settling a new country. The bachelors, of course, did not intend to stay all their lives in a country where there were no women and children. They meant to make some money as quickly as they could and then go back to England to live. The married men who had left their families behind them were in still greater haste to make what they could and go home. In short, for a dozen years after the colony was planted, nobody thought of it as his real home, where he meant to live out his life. If the colonists had been married men, with wives and children in Virginia, they would have done all they could to make the new settlement a pleasant one to live in: they would have built good houses, set up schools, and worked hard to improve their own fortunes and to keep order in the colony.

But year after year the ships brought cargoes of single men to Virginia, and the settlement was scarcely more than a camp in the woods. After the company had been trying for a good many years to people a new country by landing shiploads of bachelors on its shores, it began to dawn upon their minds that if the Virginia settlement was ever to grow into a thriving and lasting colony, there must be women and children there to make happy homes, as well as men to raise wheat, corn, and tobacco.

Sir Edwin Sandys was the wise man who saw all this most clearly. He urged the company to send out hard-working married men, who would take their wives and children with them to Virginia and settle there for good. But this was not all. There were already a great many bachelors in the colony, and there were no young women there for them to marry. Sir Edwin knew that if these bachelors were to stay in Virginia and become prosperous colonists they must have a chance to marry and set up homes of their own. So he went to work in England to get together a cargo of sweethearts for the colonists. He persuaded ninety young women of good character to go out in one of the company's ships, to marry young men in Virginia.

The plan was an odd one, but it was managed with good sense and did well for everybody concerned. It was agreed that the company should provide the young women with such clothing and other things as they would need for the voyage, and should give them free passage on board the ship. When they landed in Virginia they were to be perfectly free to marry or not, as they pleased. If any of them did not at once find husbands to their liking they were to be provided for in good homes until they chose to marry.

But no man could marry one of these young women without paying for her in tobacco, which was used instead of money in Virginia. The girls were not to be sold, exactly, but it was expected that each colonist who married one of them should pay the company as much as it had spent in bringing her across the ocean.

And the men of the colony were glad enough to do this. When the shipload of sweethearts landed at Jamestown a large number of men who were tired of bachelor life hurried to the wharf to get wives for themselves if they could. They went among the young maids, introduced themselves, got acquainted, and did all the courting that was necessary in a very little time. The young women were honest, good, well-brought-up girls, and among the many men there were plenty of good, industrious, and brave fellows who wanted good wives, and so all the girls were "engaged" at once. The men paid down one hundred and twenty pounds of tobacco apiece—for that was the price fixed upon—and, as there was nothing to wait for, the clergymen were sent for and the weddings took place immediately.

It was an odd thing to do, of course, but the circumstances were very unusual, and the plan of importing sweethearts by the cargo really seems to have been a very good one. It must have been a strange sight when the girls landed and met the men who had come to the town to woo and marry them. And many of the girls must have felt that they took great risks in coming three thousand miles from home and marrying men whom they had known for so short a time; but it seems that the marriages were happy ones, in spite of the haste in which they were made. The newly-married pairs went to work in earnest to create good homes for themselves, and when their English friends learned from their letters how happy and prosperous they were, another company of sixty sweethearts set sail for the colony and became the wives of good men.

It was in this way that the English camp at Jamestown was changed into a real colony of people who meant to live in America and to build up a thriving community here. Now that the men had wives and children to provide for, they no longer lived "from hand to mouth," hoping to make a fortune by some lucky stroke, and then to leave the colony forever. They went to work, instead, to cultivate the land, to build good houses, to make and save money, to educate their children, and to become prosperous and happy in their homes. Virginia, which had been a mere stopping-place to them, was now their own country, where their families lived and their nearest friends were around them. There they expected to pass their lives in efforts to better their own fortunes, and to make the country a pleasant one for their children and grandchildren after them to live in. They were anxious to have schools and churches, and to keep up right standards of morals and proper manners in the colony, so that their children might grow to be good and happy men and women.

That is the way in which the first English colony in America became prosperous, and many of the men who afterwards became famous in the history of the nation were the great-great-grandsons of the women whom Sir Edwin Sandys sent out as sweethearts for the colonists.

The Pilgrims, who settled at Plymouth about the time that all this happened, brought their families with them, and quickly made themselves at home in America. The planting of these two colonies—the first in Virginia and the second in Massachusetts—was the beginning from which our great, free, and happy country, with its fifty millions of people, has grown.

THE BOYHOOD OF DANIEL WEBSTER.[A]

Daniel Webster, the great statesman, orator, and lawyer, was born on the 18th of January, 1782.

His father lived near the head-waters of the Merrimac River, and the only school within reach was a poor one kept open for a few months every winter. There Webster learned all that the country schoolmaster could teach him, which was very little; but he acquired a taste which did more for him than the reading, writing, and arithmetic of the school. He learned to like books, and to want knowledge; and when a boy gets really hungry and thirsty for knowledge it is not easy to keep him ignorant. When some of the neighbors joined in setting up a little circulating library, young Webster read every book in it two or three times, and even committed to memory a large part of the best of them. It was this eagerness for education on his part that led his father afterwards to send him to Exeter to school, and later to put him into Dartmouth College.

There are not many boys in our time who have not declaimed parts of Webster's great speeches; and it will interest them to know that the boy who afterwards made those speeches could never declaim at all while he was at school. He learned his pieces well, and practised them in his own room, but he could not speak them before people to save his life.

Webster was always fond of shooting and fishing, and, however hard he studied, the people around him called him lazy and idle, because he would spend whole days in these sports. Once, while he was studying under Dr. Woods to prepare for college, that gentleman spoke to him on the subject, and hurt his feelings a little. The boy went to his room determined to have revenge, and this is the way he took to get it. The usual Latin lesson was one hundred lines of Virgil, but Webster spent the whole night over the book. The next morning before breakfast he went to Dr. Woods and read the whole lesson correctly. Then he said:

"Will you hear a few more lines, doctor?"

The teacher consenting, Webster read on and on and on, while the breakfast grew cold. Still there was no sign of the boy's stopping, and the hungry doctor at last asked how much farther he was prepared to read.

"To the end of the twelfth book of the Æneid," answered the "idle" boy, in triumph.

After that, Webster did not give up his hunting and fishing, but he worked so hard at his lessons, and got on so fast, that there was no further complaint of his "idleness." He not only learned the lessons given to him, but more, every day, and besides this he read every good book he could lay his hands on, for he was not at all satisfied to know only what could be found in the school-books.

Webster's father was poor and in debt, but finding how eager his boy was for education, and seeing, too, that he possessed unusual ability, he determined, ill as he could afford the expense, to send him to college. Accordingly, young Daniel went to Dartmouth.

Many anecdotes are told to illustrate the character of young Dan. He was always lavish of his money when he had any, while his brother was careful but generous, especially to Dan, whom he greatly admired. On one occasion the boys went to a neighboring town on a high holiday, each with a quarter of a dollar in his pocket.

"Well, Dan," said the father on their return, "what did you do with your money?"

"Spent it," answered the boy.

"And what did you do with yours, Zeke?"

"Lent it to Dan," was the answer. The fact was that Dan had spent both quarters.

Young Webster was very industrious in his studies, as we have seen, and he was physically strong and active as his fondness for sport proved; but he could never endure farm-work. One day his father wanted him to help him in cutting hay with a scythe; but very soon the boy complained that the scythe was not "hung" to suit him; that is to say, it was not set at a proper angle upon its handle. The old gentleman, adjusted it, but still it did not suit the boy. After repeated attempts to arrange it to Dan's liking, the father said, impatiently, "Well, hang it to suit yourself." And young Dan immediately "hung" it over a branch of an apple-tree and left it there. That was the hanging which pleased him.

"'TO THE END OF THE TWELFTH BOOK OF THE ÆNEID,' ANSWERED THE 'IDLE' BOY, IN TRIUMPH."

After finishing his college course Webster began studying law, but having no money, and being unwilling to tax his father for further support, he went into Northern Maine, and taught school there for a time. While teaching he devoted his evenings to the work of copying deeds and other legal documents, and by close economy managed to live upon the money thus earned, thus saving the whole of his salary as a teacher. With this money to live on, he went to Boston, studied law, and soon distinguished himself. The story of his life as a public man, in the senate, in the cabinet, and at the bar, is well known, and does not belong to this sketch of his boyhood.

THE SCULLION WHO BECAME A SCULPTOR.

In the little Italian village of Possagno there lived a jolly stone-cutter named Pisano. He was poor, of course, or he would not have been a stone-cutter; but he was full of good humor, and everybody liked him.

There was one little boy, especially, who loved old Pisano, and whom old Pisano loved more than anybody else in the world. This was Antonio Canova, Pisano's grandson, who had come to live with him, because his father was dead, and his mother had married a harsh man, who treated the little Antonio roughly.

Antonio was a frail little fellow, and his grandfather liked to have him near him during his working hours.

While Pisano worked at stone-cutting, little Canova played at it and at other things, such as modelling in clay, drawing, etc. The old grandfather, plain, uneducated man as he was, soon discovered that the pale-faced little fellow at his side had something more than an ordinary child's dexterity at such things.

The boy knew nothing of art or of its laws, but he fashioned his lumps of clay into forms of real beauty. His wise grandfather, seeing what this indicated, hired a teacher to give him some simple lessons in drawing, so that he might improve himself if he really had the artistic ability which the old man suspected. Pisano was much too poor, as he knew, ever to give the boy an art-education and make an artist of him, but he thought that Antonio might at least learn to be a better stone-cutter than common.

As the boy grew older he began to help in the shop during the day, while in the evening his grandmother told him stories or sang or recited poetry to him. All these things were educating him, though without his knowing it, for they were awakening his taste and stimulating his imagination, which found expression in the clay models that he loved to make in his leisure hours.

It so happened that Signor Faliero, the head of a noble Venetian family, and a man of rare understanding in art, had a place near Pisano's house, and at certain seasons the nobleman entertained many distinguished guests there. When the palace was very full of visitors, old Pisano was sometimes hired to help the servants with their tasks, and the boy Canova, when he was twelve years old, sometimes did scullion's work there, also, for a day, when some great feast was given.

On one of these occasions, when the Signor Faliero was to entertain a very large company at dinner, young Canova was at work over the pots and pans in the kitchen. The head-servant made his appearance, just before the dinner hour, in great distress.

The man who had been engaged to furnish the great central ornament for the table had, at the last moment, sent word that he had spoiled the piece. It was now too late to secure another, and there was nothing to take its place. The great vacant space in the centre of the table spoiled the effect of all that had been done to make the feast artistic in appearance, and it was certain that Signor Faliero would be sorely displeased.

But what was to be done? The poor fellow whose business it was to arrange the table was at his wits' end.

While every one stood dismayed and wondering, the begrimed scullion boy timidly approached the distressed head-servant, and said, "If you will let me try, I think I can make something that will do."

"You!" exclaimed the servant; "and who are you?"

"I am Antonio Canova, Pisano's grandson," answered the pale-faced little fellow.

"And what can you do, pray?" asked the man, in astonishment at the conceit of the lad.

"I can make you something that will do for the middle of the table," said the boy, "if you'll let me try."

The servant had little faith in the boy's ability, but not knowing what else to do, he at last consented that Canova should try.

Calling for a large quantity of butter, little Antonio quickly modelled a great crouching lion, which everybody in the kitchen pronounced beautiful, and which the now rejoicing head-servant placed carefully upon the table.

The company that day consisted of the most cultivated men of Venice— merchants, princes, noblemen, artists, and lovers of art—and among them were many who, like Faliero himself, were skilled critics of artwork.

When these people were ushered in to dinner their eyes fell upon the butter lion, and they forgot for what purpose they had entered the dining-room. They saw there something of higher worth in their eyes than any dinner could be, namely, a work of genius.

They scanned the butter lion critically, and then broke forth in a torrent of praises, insisting that Faliero should tell them at once what great sculptor he had persuaded to waste his skill upon a work in butter, that must quickly melt away. But Signor Faliero was as ignorant as they, and he had, in his turn, to make inquiry of the chief servant.

When the company learned that the lion was the work of a scullion, Faliero summoned the boy, and the banquet became a sort of celebration in his honor.

But it was not enough to praise a lad so gifted. These were men who knew that such genius as his belonged to the world, not to a village, and it was their pleasure to bring it to perfection by educating the boy in art. Signor Faliero himself claimed the right to provide for young Antonio, and at once declared his purpose to defray the lad's expenses, and to place him under the tuition of the best masters.

The boy whose highest ambition had been to become a village stone-cutter, and whose home had been in his poor old grandfather's cottage, became at once a member of Signor Faliero's family, living in his palace, having everything that money could buy at his command, and daily receiving instruction from the best sculptors of Venice.

But he was not in the least spoiled by this change in his fortunes. He remained simple, earnest, and unaffected. He worked as hard to acquire knowledge and skill in art as he had meant to work to become a dexterous stone-cutter.

Antonio Canova's career from the day on which he moulded the butter into a lion was steadily upward; and when he died, in 1822, he was not only one of the most celebrated sculptors of his time, but one of the greatest, indeed, of all time.

THE BOYHOOD OF WILLIAM CHAMBERS.

Boys and girls who can buy attractive periodicals and books at any bookstore or news-stand, can have very little notion of the difficulty that little folk had seventy or eighty years ago in getting something to read. It was only about fifty years ago, indeed, that this first efforts were made to supply cheap, instructive, and entertaining literature, and one of the men who made those efforts was Mr. William Chambers, who, in 1882, when he was eighty-two years of age, published a little account of his life. What he has to tell of his boyhood and youth is very interesting.

His father was unfortunate in business, and became so poor that young Chambers had to begin making his own way very early in life. He had little schooling—only six pounds' (thirty dollars) worth in all, he tells us—and, as there were no juvenile books or periodicals in those days, and no books of any other kind, except costly ones, it was hard for him to do much in the way of educating himself. But William Chambers meant to learn all that he could, and that determination counted for a good deal. There was a small circulating library in his native town, and he began by reading all the books in it, without skipping one. Then he got hold of a copy of the "Encyclopædia Britannica," which most boys would regard as very dry reading. He read it carefully. When that was done young Chambers was really pretty well educated, although he did not know it.

About that time the boy had to go to work for his living. He became an apprentice to a bookseller in Edinburgh. His wages were only four shillings (about a dollar) a week, and on that small sum he had to support himself, paying for food, lodging, clothes, and everything else, for five years. "It was a hard but somewhat droll scrimmage with semistarvation," he says; for, after paying for his lodgings and clothes, he had only about seven cents a day with which to buy his food.

In the summer he jumped out of bed at five o'clock every morning, and spent the time before the hour for beginning business in reading and making electrical experiments. He studied French in that way too, and on Sundays carried a French Testament to church, and read in French what the minister read in English.

Winter came on, and the poor lad was puzzled. It was not only cold, but entirely dark at five o'clock in the morning during the winter months, and William, who had only seven cents a day to buy food with, could not afford either a fire or a candle to read by. There was no other time of day, however, that he could call his own, and so it seemed that he must give up his reading altogether, which was a great grief to the ambitious lad.

Just then a piece of good-luck befell him. He happened to know what is called a "sandwich man"—that is to say, a man who walks about with signs hanging behind and before him. One day this man made him a proposition. The sandwich man knew a baker who, with his two sons, carried on a small business in a cellar. The baker was fond of reading, but had no time for it, and as he and his sons had to bake their bread early in the morning, he proposed, through the sandwich man, to employ William Chambers as reader. His plan was that Chambers should go to the cellar bakery every morning at five o'clock and read to the bakers, and for this service he promised to give the boy one hot roll each morning. Here was double good-fortune. It enabled Chambers to go on with his reading by the baker's light and fire, and it secured for him a sufficient breakfast without cost.

He accepted the proposition at once, and for two and a half hours every morning he sat on a flour-sack in the cellar, and read to the bakers by the light of a penny candle stuck in a bottle.

Out of his small wages it was impossible for the boy to save anything, and so, when the five years of his apprenticeship ended, he had only five shillings in the world. Yet he determined to begin business at once on his own account. Getting credit for ten pounds' worth of books, he opened a little stall, and thus began what has since grown to be a great publishing business.

He had a good deal of unoccupied time at his stall, and "in order to pick up a few shillings," as he says, he began to write out neat copies of poems for albums. Finding sale for these, he determined to enlarge that part of his business by printing the poems. For that purpose he bought a small and very "squeaky" press and a font of worn type which had been used for twenty years. He had to teach himself how to set the type, and, as his press would print only half a sheet at a time, it was very slow work; but he persevered, and gradually built up a little printing business in connection with his book-selling. After a while he published an edition of Burns's poems, setting the type, printing the pages, and binding the books with his own hands, and clearing eight pounds by the work.

Chambers wrote a good deal at that time, and his brother Robert wrote still more, so that they were at once authors, printers, publishers, and booksellers, but all in a very small way. After ten years of this work, William Chambers determined to publish a cheap weekly paper, to be filled with entertaining and instructive matters, designed especially for the people who could not afford to buy expensive books and periodicals. Robert refused to join in this scheme, and so, for a time, the whole work and risk fell upon

William. His friends all agreed in thinking that ruin would be the result; but William Chambers thought he knew what the people wanted, and hence he went on.

The result soon justified his expectations. The first number was published on the 4th of February, 1832. Thirty thousand copies were sold in a few days, and three weeks later the sale rose to fifty thousand copies a week.

HOW A BOY WAS HIRED OUT, AND WHAT CAME OF IT.

When Michael Angelo was twelve years of age, although he had had no instruction in art, he did a piece of work which greatly pleased the painter Domenico Ghirlandajo. That artist at once declared that here was lad of genius, who must quit his school studies and become a painter.

This was what the little Michael most wished to do, but he had no hope that his father would listen for a moment to the suggestion. His father, Ludovico Buonarotti, was a distinguished man in the state, and held art and artists in contempt. He had planned a great political career for his boy, as the boy knew very well.

Ghirlandajo was enthusiastic, however, and, in company with the lad, he at once visited Ludovico, and asked him to place Michael in his studio.

Ludovico was very angry, saying that he wished his son to become a prominent man in society and politics, not a dauber and a mason; but when he found that young Michael was determined to be an artist or nothing he gave way, though most ungraciously. He would not say that he consented to place his son with Ghirlandajo; he would not admit that the study of art was study, or the studio of an artist anything but a shop. He said to the artist: "I give up my son to you. He shall be your apprentice or your servant, as you please, for three years, and you must pay me twenty-four florins for his services."

In spite of the insulting words and the insulting terms, Michael Angelo consented thus to be hired out as a servant to the artist, who should have been paid by his father for teaching him. He had to endure much, indeed, besides the anger and contempt of his father, who forbade him even to visit his house, and utterly disowned him. His fellow-pupils were jealous of his ability, and ill-treated him constantly, one of them going so far as to break his nose with a blow.

When Michael Angelo had been with Ghirlandajo about two years, he went one day to the Gardens of St. Mark, where the Prince Lorenzo de' Medici—who was the foremost patron of art in Florence—had established a rich museum of art-works at great expense. One of the workmen in the garden gave the boy leave to try his hand at copying some of the sculptures there, and Michael, who had hitherto studied only painting, was glad of a chance to experiment with the chisel, which he preferred to the brush. He chose for his model an ancient figure of a faun, which was somewhat mutilated. The mouth, indeed, was entirely broken off, but the boy was very self-reliant, and this did not trouble him. He worked day after day at the piece, creating a mouth for it of his own imagining, with the lips parted in laughter and the teeth displayed.

When he had finished, and was looking at his work, a man standing near asked if he might offer a criticism.

"Yes," answered the boy, "if it is a just one."

"Of that you shall be the judge," said the man.

"Very well. What is it?"

"The forehead of your faun is old, but the mouth is young. See, it has a full set of perfect teeth. A faun so old as this one is would not have perfect teeth."

The lad admitted the justice of the criticism, and proceeded to remedy the defect by chipping away two or three of the teeth, and chiselling the gums so as to give them a shrivelled appearance.

The next morning, when Michael went to remove his faun from the garden, it was gone. He searched everywhere for it, but without success. Finally, seeing the man who had made the suggestion about the teeth, he asked him if he knew where it was.

"Yes," replied the man, "and if you will follow me I'll show you where it is."

"Will you give it back to me? I made it, and have a right to it."

"Oh, if you must have it, you shall."

With that he led the way into the palace of the prince, and there, among the most precious works of art in the collection, stood the faun. The young sculptor cried out in alarm, declaring that the Prince Lorenzo would never forgive the introduction of so rude a piece of work among his treasures of sculpture. To his astonishment the man declared that he was himself the Prince Lorenzo de' Medici, and that he set the highest value upon this work.

"I am your protector and friend," he added. "Henceforth you shall be counted as my son, for you are destined to become one of the great masters of art."

This was overwhelming good-fortune. Lorenzo de' Medici was a powerful nobleman, known far and wide to be a most expert judge of works of art. His approval was in itself fame and fortune.

Filled with joy, the lad went straightway to his father's house, which he had been forbidden to enter, and, forcing his way into Ludovico's presence, told him what had happened. The father refused to believe the good news until Michael led him into Lorenzo's presence.

When the prince, by way of emphasizing his goodwill, offered Ludovico any post he might choose, he asked for a very modest place indeed, saying, with bitter contempt, that it was good enough "for the father of a mason."

THE WICKEDEST MAN IN THE WORLD.

Precisely at what time the faithful and affectionate subjects of his Majesty Ivan IV., Czar of all the Russias, conferred upon him his pet name, "The Terrible," history neglects to inform us, but we are left in no uncertainty as to the entire appropriateness of the title, which is now inseparably linked with his baptismal name. He inherited the throne at the age of three years, and his early education was carefully attended to by his faithful guardians, who snubbed and scared him, in the hope that they might so far weaken his intellect as to secure a permanent control over him, and through him govern Russia as they pleased. They made a footstool of him sometimes, and a football at others, and, under their system of training, the development of those qualities of mind and heart for which he is celebrated was remarkably rapid. He was always Ivan the Terrified, and he became Ivan the Terrible before he was old enough to have played a reasonably good game of marbles, or to have become tolerably expert in the art of mumbling the peg. Indeed, it seems that the young grand-prince was wholly insensible to the joys of these and the other excellent sports in which ordinary youths delight, and being of an ingenious turn of mind, he invented others better suited to his tastes and character. One of these pastimes—perhaps the first and simplest one devised by the youthful genius—consisted in the dropping of cats, dogs, and other domestic animals from the top of the palace to the pavement below, and sentimental historians have construed these interesting experiments in the law of gravitation into acts of wanton cruelty. Another of the young czar's amusements was to turn half-famished pet bears loose upon passing pedestrians, and it is the part of charity to suppose that his purpose in this was to study the psychological and physiognomical phenomena of fear. A less profitable way be had of accomplishing the same thing was by throwing, or, as youthful Americans phrase it, "shying," stones at passers-by, concealing himself meanwhile behind a screen. He cultivated his skill in horsemanship by riding over elderly people, cripples, and children. In short, his boyish sports were all of an original and highly interesting sort.

Up to the age of thirteen Ivan was under the tutelage of a council, of which the Prince Shnisky was chief, and it was this prince who domineered over the boy and made a footstool and a football of his body. At that age Ivan asserted his independence in a very positive and emphatic way, which even the Prince Shnisky could not misapprehend. The young czar was out hunting, accompanied by Shnisky and other princes and boyards, among whom was Prince Gluisky, a rival of Shnisky's, who was prejudiced against that excellent gentleman. At his suggestion, Ivan addressed his guardian Shnisky in language which the latter deemed insolent. Shnisky replied angrily, and Ivan requested his dogs to remonstrate with the prince, which they did by tearing him limb from limb.

Having thus silenced the dictation of Shnisky, the young prince became the ward of the no less excellent Gluisky, and was carefully taught that the only way in which he could effectually assert authority was by punishment. It was made clear to his budding intellect, too, that the shortest, simplest, and altogether the best way to get rid of disagreeable persons was to put them to death, and throughout his life Ivan never forgot this lesson for a single moment. Power, he was told, was worthless unless it was used, and the only way in which it could be really used was by oppression. For three years no pains were spared to teach him this system of ethics and politics, and the young prince, in his anxiety to perfect himself in the art of governing, diligently practised all these precepts.

When he was seventeen years of age he was formally crowned czar. The citizens, ignorant of the truths of political economy and the principles of governmental science underlying the young Czar's system, became alarmed, and fired the city one night. When Ivan awoke, he was terrified, being of an abnormally nervous temperament, and the apparition of a warning monk, together with the influence of Anastasia, the young czarina, led the czar to abandon the simple and straightforward methods of government in which he had been bred, and for thirteen years, under the dictation of Alexis Adascheff and the monk Sylvester, Ivan devoted himself to the commonplace employments of developing Russia politically and socially. He dismissed his ministers and put others in their places. He reorganized the army; revised the code, in the interest of abstract justice; equalized assessments; subdued the Tartars; established forts for the protection of the frontiers; laid the foundation for the future greatness of his empire; began the work which was completed so grandly under Peter the Great; introduced printing into Russia; added greatly to her possessions; checked the abuses of the clergy; brought artists from western Europe, and in a hundred ways made himself famous by doing those things which historians love to chronicle.

Meanwhile, his genius for governing upon the Gluiskian system lay dormant. It was not dead, but slept, and after its nap of thirteen years it awoke one day, refreshed. Anastasia, the beautiful queen whose influence had been supreme for so long a time, died, and Ivan was free again. He recalled an old bishop who had been banished for his crimes, and consulted him as to his future course.

"If you wish to be truly a sovereign," said this eminent prelate, "never seek a counsellor wiser than yourself; never receive advice from any man. Command, but never obey; and you will be a terror to the boyards. Remember that he who is permitted to begin by advising is certain to end by ruling his sovereign."

Here was advice of a sort suited to Ivan's taste and education, and for reply he kissed the good bishop's hand, saying:

"My own father could not have spoken more wisely."

That the czar spoke sincerely, his faithfulness in following the bishop's precepts abundantly attests.

His ministers and advisers being manifestly wiser than he, and therefore not at all the proper kind of people to have about, he straightway banished them. He then began a diligent search for their partisans, some of whom he put to death, condemning others to imprisonment and torture. He next turned his attention to his own household, which he was resolved upon ruling absolutely, at least, if not well. One of the princes made himself disagreeable by declining to participate freely in the pleasures of the palace, and, for the sake of domestic harmony, Ivan had him poniarded while he was at his prayers. Another so far overstepped the bounds of courtesy and propriety as to remonstrate with one of the new favorites upon his improper conduct, and Ivan, in order that there might be no bickerings and hard feelings in his family, slew the discourteous prince with his own hand.

He was in the habit of carrying an iron rod about with him, and he had a playful way of striking his friends with it now and then, merely for his amusement. His pleasantries of this and like sorts were endless. One day Prince Boris, a boyard, came to pay his respects to the czar, and as be bowed to the ground, according to custom, Ivan, seizing a knife, said, "God bless thee, my dear Boris; thou deservest a proof of my favor," and with that he kindly cut the nobleman's ear off.

When Prince Kurbsky, whom he had threatened with death, fled to Poland and wrote him a letter thence, telling him pretty plainly what he thought of him, the czar playfully struck the bearer of the missive with his iron rod, as a preliminary to the reading of the letter, and the blood flowed copiously from the man's wounds while Ivan pondered the words of his rebellious subject. He then became convinced that the boyards generally sympathized with Kurbsky, and to teach them better he put a good many of them to death by torture, and deprived many others of their estates. His alarm was very real, however, for he was a phenomenon of abject cowardice. He therefore fled to a fortified place in the midst of a dense forest, where he remained a month, writing letters to the Russians, telling them that he had abdicated and left them to their fate as a punishment for their disloyalty and their crimes. Singularly enough, his flight terrified the people. He had taught them that he was their god as God was his, and his flight to Alexandrovsky seemed to them a withdrawal of the protection of Providence itself. Business was suspended. The courts ceased to sit. The country was in an agony of terror. A large deputation of boyards and priests journeyed to Alexandrovsky, and besought the sovereign to return and resume his holy functions as the head of the church, that the souls of so many millions might not perish. Exacting of clergy and nobles an admission of his absolute right to do as he pleased, and a promise that they would in no way interfere with or resist his authority, he returned to Moscow. Here he surrounded himself with a body-guard of desperadoes, one thousand strong at first, and afterwards increased to six thousand, whose duty it was to discover the czar's enemies and to sweep them from the face of the earth. As emblems of these their functions, each member of the guard carried at his saddle-bow a dog's head and a broom. As the punishment of the czar's enemies included the confiscation of their property, a large part of which was given to the guards themselves, these were always singularly successful in discovering the disaffection of wealthy nobles, finding it out oftentimes before the nobles themselves were aware of their own treasonable sentiments.

Feeling unsafe still, Ivan built for himself a new palace, outside the walls of the Kremlin, making it an impregnable castle. Then, finding that even this did not lull his shaken nerves to rest, he proceeded to put danger afar off by dispossessing the twelve thousand rich nobles whose estates lay nearest the palace, and giving their property to his personal followers, so that the head which wore the crown might lie easy in the conviction that there were no possible enemies near on the other side of the impregnable walls which shut him in. But even then he could not sleep easily, and so he repaired again to his forest stronghold at Alexandrovsky, where he surrounded himself with guards and ramparts. Here he converted the palace into a monastery, made himself abbot, and his rascally followers monks. He rigorously enforced monastic observances of the severest sort, and no doubt became a saint, in his own estimation. He spent most of his time at prayers, allowing himself no recreation except a daily sight of the torture of the prisoners who were confined in the dungeons of the fortress. His guards were allowed rather a larger share of amusement, and they wandered from street to street during the day, punishing, with their hatchets, such disloyal persons as they encountered. They were very moderate in their indulgences, however, in imitation of their sovereign, doubtless, and it is recorded to their credit, that, at this time, they rarely killed more than twenty people in one day, while sometimes the number was as low as five.

But a quiet life of this kind could not always content the czar. Naturally, he grew tired of individual killings, and began to long for some more exciting sport. When, one day, a quarrel arose between some of his guards and a few of the people of Torjek, Ivan saw at a glance that all the inhabitants of Torjek were mutinous rebels, and of course it became his duty to put them all to death, which he straightway did.

Up to this time the genius of Ivan seems to have been cautiously feeling its way, and so the part of his history already sketched may be regarded as a mere preliminary to his real career. His extraordinary capacity for ruling an empire upon the principles taught him by the Prince Gluisky was now about to show itself in all its greatness. A criminal of Novgorod, feeling himself aggrieved by the authorities of that city, who had incarcerated him for a time, wrote a letter offering to place the city under Polish protection. This letter he signed, not with his own name, but with that of the archbishop, and, instead of sending it to the King of Poland, to whom it was addressed, he secreted it in the church of St. Sophia. Then, going to Alexandrovsky, he told Ivan that treason was contemplated by the Novgorodians, and that the treasonable letter would be found behind the statue of the Virgin in the church. Ivan sent a messenger to find the letter, and upon his return the czar began his march upon the doomed city. Happening to pass through the town of Khur, on his way to Novgorod, he put all its inhabitants to death, with the purpose, doubtless, of training his troops in the art of wholesale massacre, before requiring them to practise it upon the people of Novgorod. Finding this system of drill an agreeable pastime, he repeated it upon his arrival at the city of Twer, and then, in order that the other towns along his route might have no reason to complain of partiality, he bestowed upon all of them a like manifestation of his imperial regard.

It is not my purpose to describe in detail the elaborate and ingenious cruelty practised in the massacre of the Novgorodians. The story is sickening. Ivan first heard mass, and then began the butchery, which lasted for many days, was conducted with the utmost deliberation and most ingenious cruelty, and ended in the slaughter of sixty thousand people. Ivan had selected certain prominent citizens, to the number of several hundred, whom he reserved for public and particularly cruel execution at Moscow. Summoning the small and wretched remnant of the population to his presence, he besought their prayers for the continuance and prosperity of his reign, and with gracious words of farewell took his departure from the city.

The execution in Moscow of the reserved victims was a scene too horrible to be described in these pages. Indeed, the half of Ivan's enormities may not be told here at all, and even the historians content themselves with the barest outlines of many parts of his career. He thought himself in some sense a deity, and blasphemously asserted that his throne was surrounded by archangels precisely as God's is. Identifying himself with the Almighty, he claimed exemption from the observance of God's laws, and, in defiance of the fundamental principles of the Greek Church, of which he was the head, he married seven wives. Believing that he might with equal impunity insult the moral sense of other nations, he actually sought to add England's queen, Elizabeth, to the list of his spouses. And he was so far right in his estimate of his power to do as he pleased, that the Virgin Queen, head of the English Church, while she would not herself become one of his wives, consented to assist him, and selected for his eighth consort Mary Hastings, the daughter of the Earl of Huntingdon. She came near bringing about a marriage between the two, in face of the fact that the two churches of which Ivan and she were respectively the heads were agreed in condemning polygamy as a heinous crime.

For one only of all his crimes Ivan showed regret, if not remorse. His oldest and favorite son, when the city of Pskof was besieged by the Poles, asked that he might be intrusted with the command of a body of troops with which to assist the beleaguered place. Ivan was so great a coward that he dared not trust the affection and loyalty of even his own favorite child, and in a fit of mingled fear and rage he beat the young man to death with his iron staff, saying, "Rebel, you are leagued with the boyards in a conspiracy to dethrone me."

Remorse seized upon him at once, and his sufferings and his fears of retribution were terrible. Finally he determined to abandon the throne and seek peace in a convent, but the infatuated Russians entreated him not to desert them. He died at last, in 1580.

Did Scheherazade herself ever imagine a stranger story than this? And yet it is plain history, and is only a fragment of the truth.

A PRINCE WHO WOULD NOT STAY DEAD.

His name was Dmitri, and he was hereditary Grand-Prince of all the Russias, being the son of Ivan the Terrible, and only surviving brother of Feodor, the childless successor of that blood-thirsty czar. He was carefully killed in the presence of witnesses, during his boyhood, and duly buried, with honors appropriate to his station in life; so that if Dmitri had been an ordinary mortal, or even an ordinary prince, there would have been no story of his life to tell, except the brief tragedy of his taking off. He was no ordinary prince, however, and so the trifling incident of his death during childhood had as little to do with his career as had one or two other episodes of a like nature in the history of his later life. He was born to rule Russia, and was not at all disposed to excuse himself from the performance of the duty Providence had thus imposed upon him, by pleading the two or three thorough killings to which he was subjected. The story, as preserved in authentic history, is a very interesting one, and may perhaps bear repeating here. The reader may find all the facts in any reputable history of Russia, or of the houses of Rurik and Romanoff.

In his jealousy of the absolute power he wielded, Ivan the Terrible had made constant war upon his nobility—killing them, or driving them away, and in every way possible destroying whatever share of influence they possessed in the state. When he died, leaving as his successor Feodor, a weak prince, of uncertain temper and infirm intellect, the nobility—naturally enough—hoped to regain their ancient influence in the state, and might have accomplished their purpose without difficulty if their measures to that end had been taken concertedly; but, jealous as they were of the privileges of their class, they were even more tenacious of their individual and family pretensions. They quarrelled among themselves, in short, and, while they were quarrelling, a bold and ambitious man, Boris Godunof, who happened to be the czar's brother-in-law, conceived the project of becoming prime-minister and actual ruler of the empire. Indeed, his ambition extended even further than this. Not content with governing Russia in the name of Feodor, he set covetous eyes upon the purple itself, and was resolved to become czar in name as well as in fact. But this was a delicate and difficult task, and could by accomplished only at great risk and by great patience. Boris was a man of undoubted genius, extreme shrewdness, unlimited ambition, and remarkable personal courage; and difficult and dangerous as his task was, he seems never to have faltered in his purpose from the instant of its conception to the time of its execution.

Knowing the power of money in state affairs, he took care to accumulate a vast sum in his own private coffers, as a first step. He conciliated the common people in a hundred ways—by wise legislation, by the reformation of abuses which pressed hardly upon them, and sometimes by the oppression of the nobles in the interest of the lower classes. He was not long in making himself altogether the most popular man in Russia. He removed, by death or banishment, those whom he could not conciliate, together with all other persons whom he thought likely to prove obstacles in the way of his grand purpose. In short, a very brief time sufficed him for the winning of a popularity which, in any country but Russia, would have been sufficient for his need. But Boris knew his Russians well. He knew that loyalty to the line of Rurik was the strongest feeling in their breasts, after that of devotion to their creed—of which, indeed, it formed a chief part. It was their fixed belief in the divine right of the legitimate princes of the House of Rurik to reign, that had kept them patient, even under the rigors of Ivan's rule; and Boris knew well enough that no usurper, however strongly intrenched in their affections he might be, could hope to win those superstitiously loyal people to his support against any prince of the right line, however brutal, unjust, and despotic that prince might be. He knew, in brief, that so long as any descendant of Rurik should live, no other man could hope to seat himself upon the Muscovite throne. Feodor had no children, but he had one brother, the lad Dmitri, who would be his successor in the natural course of events. His existence was sure to prove an effectual bar to all Boris's hopes; and so it was necessary to get him out of the way before the scheme should be ripe for execution. To accomplish this, the wily minister sent Dmitri and his mother to the distant town of Uglitch, and there, by his orders, the young prince was murdered, in the presence of his nurse and six other people, and buried from his mother's residence. This was in 1591. The lad's death was announced, of course. Indeed, it was known to nearly everybody in Uglitch, the tocsin having been sounded, and the population having gathered around the murdered boy, where they put to death a good many who were suspected of complicity with the murderers. But in publishing it abroad in Russia, Boris deemed it prudent to attribute it, some say to a fever, others to an accidental fall upon a knife with which the boy had been playing; and lest the people of Uglitch should embarrass the minister by insisting upon a different diagnosis of the boy's last illness, that prudent official put a great many of them to death, cut the tongues out of others' heads, and banished the rest to Siberia—laying the town in ashes. He spared the lad's mother, but shut her up in a convent.

Dmitri was now out of the way, or, rather, he would have been if he had had an ordinary capacity for staying comfortably killed; and Boris redoubled his efforts to prepare the way for his own elevation to the throne, as Feodor's successor, when that prince should chance to let the sceptre fall from his grasp.

To secure the influence of the Church in his behalf, he bought of a Greek bishop the right to appoint the successor of the patriarch (a sort of Greek Church pope); and that office presently becoming vacant, he appointed a creature of his own as head of the Church. He succeeded in winning the favor of the inferior nobility, who were very numerous, and made himself strong in many other ways.

Boris was a fellow of infinite good-luck; and so it fell out that, at the precise moment when all his plans were complete, the Czar Feodor obligingly died. So opportunely did this event happen, that grave historians have been inclined to suspect Boris of having procured it in some way; but of this there is no positive evidence.

Feodor dead, there was no heir to the throne. With him ended the line of Rurik, which alone the Russians recognized as legitimately entitled to rule the empire; and now a new czar must be chosen. The nobles quarrelled, of course. They agreed in thinking that one of their order should be elevated to the throne; but they could by no means agree which one it should be. Each resented the pretensions of all the others, and it speedily became manifest that the patriarch's nomination, upon whomsoever it might fall, would turn the scale and elect a czar. The patriarch was Boris's own creature, appointed for the sole purpose of forwarding that minister's plans; and he promptly nominated Boris to the vacant throne. The election was a prearranged affair; and presently Boris was waited upon—in the convent to which he had retired with the declared purpose of leading a monastic life in future—and informed of his selection by the people as Czar of all the Russias. He modestly declined, of course; and, equally of course, his modesty only made the people the more clamorous. After some weeks of petty dalliance Boris finally allowed himself to be persuaded, and was crowned czar, in due form, in the year 1598.

He was not long in discovering that his position was insecure, and incapable of being made safe. Whatever policy he might adopt—and he was disposed, it appears, to govern wisely and well—was sure to displease some of his subjects; and in the hands of a hostile faction, his want of hereditary claim upon the throne was a powerful weapon. What he had seized by crime he must keep by tyranny and violence, and a three years' famine added greatly to his embarrassments. Whatever he did excited discontent; and to make his wretchedness complete, he fancied himself haunted by the ghost of the murdered Dmitri. There were symptoms of mutiny everywhere, which daily threatened to culminate in open revolt. It needed only a match to fire the mine.

In 1603, when matters were at their worst, there appeared in Poland a young man who claimed to be the murdered Dmitri. His story was that, by means of an adroit substitution, another boy had been killed in his place; that he had escaped; and he claimed the throne of the Ruriks. He strongly resembled the prince he claimed to be, and his identity seemed to be established, also, by other evidence than mere personal resemblance. There was no "strawberry mark on his left arm," but both he and the dead prince, if, indeed, they were two distinct persons, had a wart on the forehead, and another under the right eye, and in both one arm was slightly longer than the other. The pretender, or real prince, as the case may be, had also a valuable jewel which had belonged to Dmitri; and so he was not long in winning credence for his story, both in Poland and in Russia. Boris gave out that the young man was the monk Otrafief, who had appeared in the army as his advocate and emissary; and some historians—Karamsin and Bell among the number—have accepted this theory; but a careful comparison of dates seems to contradict it. Whoever the man was, he was an able and accomplished diplomatist as well as a singularly bold warrior; and he succeeded presently in winning the recognition of Sigismund, King of Poland, and putting himself at the head of an army with which he invaded Russia. He had privately abjured the Greek faith, and undertaken to convert Russia into a Catholic power; and, in addition to the many other favors promised the Poles, he had engaged to marry Marina, the daughter of a Polish nobleman.

During the autumn of the year 1604, this new Dmitri began his invasion at the head of a small army made up of Poles and Don Cossacks. On his march his force was swelled by accessions, and a number of towns declared in his favor. Boris sent an army four times as great as his own, to destroy him; and battle was joined on the last day of December. Dmitri's case seemed utterly hopeless; but he was both able and brave. He fought with the resolution and courage of a hero, the skill of a consummate tactician, and the fury of a demon. And in spite of the terrible odds against him, he won a great victory. In a military way, its results were neutralized by the withdrawal of his Poles, and by some other circumstances which forbade his pushing forward towards the capital; but the moral effect was altogether in his favor. The superstitious Russians saw in his marvellous success a miracle, and accepted it as proof positive that this was the true prince, to oppose whom was sacrilege. By dint of great energy Boris was able to maintain the war till the time of his own death, which happened during the spring of 1605. His son Feodor was crowned as his successor; but a few weeks later he was deposed and strangled, and the new Dmitri came to the throne.

For a time his wisdom as a statesman promised to equal his skill and courage as a soldier, but his manifest preference for Poles to Russians soon created jealousy; and imagining that he could overcome prejudices by violent measures, as easily as he had conquered a throne, he spared no pains to insult the Russian national feeling. He appointed only Poles to high office, and lavished upon foreigners so much attention as to breed discontent in his own capital. His apostasy from the Greek to the Roman faith, also, was suspected, and the clergy became his implacable enemies. The disaffection grew daily, and the efforts Dmitri made to overawe his enemies only exasperated them. Finally, on the occasion of his marriage with Marina, the Polish princess—which was celebrated with great pomp by a throng of Polish soldiers and others, invited to Moscow for the purpose—a mob, headed by Shuiski, or Schnisky—for the name is spelled in both of these and half a dozen other ways—stormed the palace, butchered the Poles, and impaled Dmitri on a spear. To leave no doubt of his death this time, they kept his body transfixed with the spear, in front of the palace, for three days, that the people might wreak their vengeance upon the dead czar by insulting his corpse.

Schnisky profited by his victory, and while the blood of the populace was still hot was chosen czar, as successor of the impostor he had overthrown. His popularity was short-lived, however. His fellows among the nobles resented his elevation above themselves, and ere long the desire for his removal was as unanimous as his election had been. This seemed a good time for the doubly dead Dmitri to come to life again; and so it was presently rumored that after all he had not been killed; that the corpse the people had spat upon and insulted was not his; that he was alive, in Poland, and ready to claim his own. This report was industriously circulated by the nobles; but as the people had not yet forgotten their hatred for the usurper, he was permitted to lie down in his grave again.

To prevent his coming to life for a third time, the dead czar's remains were disinterred and burned. The ashes were collected and fired from a piece of artillery, and it was supposed that further resurrection on his part was impossible. But, as we have seen, Dmitri had a most astonishing genius for coming to life after being thoroughly killed; and presently he appeared again in Poland. This time, history says, he was either a Russian schoolmaster or a Polish Jew; but however that may be, certain it is that he so closely resembled the other two Dmitri's in personal appearance, even to the two warts and unequally long arms, that he imposed on everybody around him with his story. Even the Princess Marina accepted him, and actually lived with him as his wife.

He was able, without much difficulty, to interest the King of Poland in his behalf, and to secure a declaration of war by that potentate against Czar

Schnisky. He invaded Russia, won battles, captured Smolensko, invested Moscow, and finally entered the city.

About this time Dmitri appeared in several other places, but only one of him was in Moscow at the head of a victorious army; and in behalf of this particular one Schnisky resigned his crown and retired to a monastery, whence he was soon removed to a dungeon.

At this juncture the King of Poland, having plans of his own for the union of Russia and his own kingdom, withdrew his countenance from Dmitri; and that prince retired from the business of governing, and devoted himself for the rest of his life to the less honorable, but perhaps equally lucrative, profession of highway robbery. He was again killed after awhile, this time by a Don Cossack. But even this public killing had small effect. A dozen or more new Dmitri's appeared, claiming the throne; and some of them, says the historian Bell, "actually touched the sceptre for a moment, but only to recoil in fear from the dangerous object of their insane ambition."

After awhile, having found the task an unprofitable one, perhaps, Dmitri seems to have made up his mind to stay dead; but in due course a race of his sons sprang up quite as mysteriously, if not quite as persistently, to pester the Russians, and peace came to them only through the elevation of the Romanoffs to the imperial throne. Connected as they were by ties of blood with the race of Rurik, they brought legitimacy to the rescue of a land long torn by faction. The loyalty of the people to sovereigns whose right to rule was derived from Rurik, gave the dynasty a strength sufficient to maintain itself; and after a little while Peter the Great taught his Russians civilization, and a new era in Russian history was begun.

THE END.

Footnotes.

[A] For some of the materials used in this sketch I am indebted to the work entitled "The Boyhood of Great Men," by John G. Edgar, published by Messrs. Harper & Brothers.

Milton Keynes UK
Ingram Content Group UK Ltd.
UKHW030911151124
451262UK00006B/826

9 789362 995469